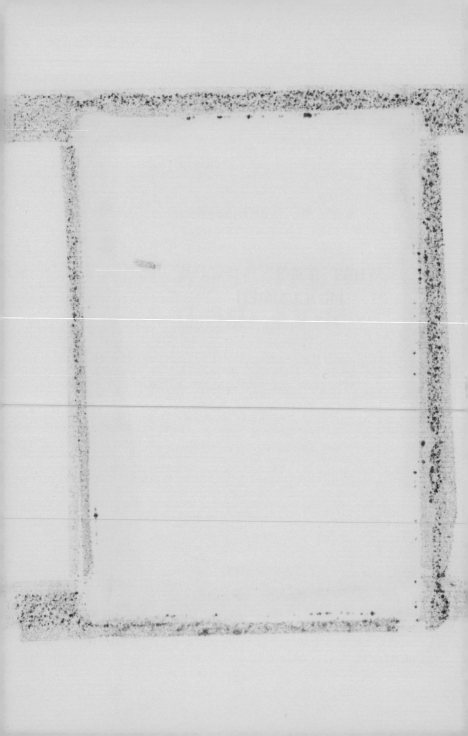

WHAT JESUS
PROCLAIMED

RAY W. RAGSDALE

WHAT JESUS PROCLAIMED

sermonic interpretations of the
basic teachings of Jesus

ABINGDON PRESS   Nashville • New York

Quotation on pages 26-27 from *The Trial of Jesus* by John Masefield. Copyright 1925 by The Macmillan Company. Used by permission.

Quotation on pages 53-54 from *Cyrano de Bergerac* by Edmund Rostand,
Brian Hooker translation. Copyright 1923 by Holt, Rinehart and Winston,
Inc. Copyright 1951 by Doris C. Hooker. Reprinted by permission of Holt,
Rinehart and Winston, Inc.

Poem on pages 77-78, "The Common Tasks," from *Songs of Hope* by Grace
Noll Crowell. Copyright 1938 by Harper & Brothers. Reprinted by permission
of Harper & Row, Publishers.

Poem on page 79 by G. K. Chesterton from *Gilbert Keith Chesterton* by
Maisie Ward. Reprinted by permission of Miss D. E. Collins and A. P. Watt
& Son.

Poem on page 123, "The Gambler," by G. A. Studdert-Kennedy. Reprinted
by permission of Harper & Row, Publishers, and Hodder and Stoughton, Ltd.

Danish hymn on pages 130-31 from *A World of Song*. Reprinted by permission of Danish American Young People's League, Grand View College, Des
Moines, Iowa.

Poem on page 135, "Outwitted," by Edwin Markham. Reprinted by permission of Virgil Markham.

Poem on page 141 by Grace Coolidge. Reprinted by permission of John
Coolidge.

SET UP, PRINTED, AND BOUND BY THE
PARTHENON PRESS, AT NASHVILLE,
TENNESSEE, UNITED STATES OF AMERICA

To Eleanor, Russell
Judy, and Merle
and
the four little girls

PREFACE

Four words enter repeatedly into the religious conversation of our time—renewal, relevance, dialogue, and unity. They are great words, and it is good that they occupy a prominent place in our thoughts.

That the church is in need of *renewal* few would question. How it is to come is another matter. Certainly one requirement is to get down to basics, and nothing could be more basic than the fundamental truths Jesus proclaimed. The church is in the process of reexamining its life, and I have faith to believe that renewal will come to the body of Christ. If it is to have lasting value, however, it must be accompanied by a searching study of the teachings of Jesus.

Again, in these days, the word *relevance* is much on our lips. It is a good word. Unless the Christian religion has meaning for our everyday existence—unless it

7

touches all the bases of human experience—people will pass it by. Nothing is more relevant to life than the ideas Jesus came to express and to embody. Mankind has looked at these ideas before, and many men have declared them to be too lofty for application. Since we have tried other ideas which seemed more practical, only to end up in despair and sometimes in disaster, it is time now to reemphasize the great teachings of Jesus and seek for their application.

We speak a great deal about *dialogue* today. We know it is important for people to talk with one another. But if this "talk" is to have any meaning, it must represent a real grappling with ideas. There is a place for small talk, but in a day when man's future is so precarious people must engage in serious dialogue as to the meaning of life and death and the whole gamut of relationships that lies between the two. If the words of Jesus are relevant, as I believe they are, nothing is more important for people to talk about today than what Jesus talked about nineteen and a half centuries ago.

We hear much about *unity* in this generation. The word "ecumenical" is no longer a strange term to our ears. The unity we seek in our ecumenical relations is not uniformity of belief and practice. What we are after is the unity that emphasizes fundamentals upon which all Christians may agree. Great strides of progress have been made as our ecumenists have engaged in serious theological dialogue. I am eager for the time when our talk will center more and more about the basic teachings of Jesus, with the nonessentials winnowed out like chaff before the wind. Our unity is in Christ, but the time must come when we spell this out in terms of what Christ proclaimed.

I am indebted to many persons in the development and preparation of this manuscript. The late Bishop G. Bromley Oxnam, as president of DePauw University before he became a bishop, inspired my first thoughtful examination of the teachings of Jesus when I was a student. Throughout my ministry I have studied and restudied them with the help of contemporary scholars. All these sermons have been preached, essentially as they appear here, to the three Sunday morning congregations of the Catalina Methodist Church of Tucson, Arizona. My secretary, Mrs. Philip Ring, has helped with research in addition to typing and retyping the manuscript. To all who have contributed to my thought in the development of these sermons, but especially to him whose ideas I have endeavored to reflect and state here, I am infinitely grateful.

Ray W. Ragsdale
Tucson, Arizona

CONTENTS

God Is
Like a Father

Philip said to him, "Lord, show us the Father, and we shall be satisfied."

—John 14:8

Rarely do we find a reference to God as a father in the Old Testament, but this word was on the lips of Jesus constantly. Whenever Jesus talked to his friends about God, he almost always used the term "Father." "My Father is working still, and I am working," said Jesus (John 5:17). And on another occasion he said, "You, therefore, must be perfect, as your heavenly Father is perfect" (Matt. 5:48).

As a boy of twelve, when his parents found him in the Temple after an anxious search, he said to them, "Did you not know that I must be in my Father's house?" (Luke 2:49). When he gave his disciples a lesson in prayer, he said, "Pray . . . like this: Our Father who art in heaven . . ." (Matt. 6:9). When the seventy returned telling of their amazing experiences, he prayed, "I thank thee, Father, Lord of heaven and earth" (Luke 10:21). The last word on the cross was, "Father, into thy hands I commit my spirit!" (Luke 23:46). Without a doubt, by word and by example, Jesus proclaimed that God is like a father.

One day when Jesus was talking with his disciples about the Father's house and how the Father could be known, there was a puzzled expression on the face of Philip. It was too much for him. He couldn't quite get it. "Lord, show us the Father, and we shall be satisfied," he said. As I picture this scene in my mind, I can see a trace of disappointment in the Master's eyes. Then, with loving patience, he says, "Have I been with you so long, and yet you do not know me, Philip? He who has seen me has seen the Father" (John 14:9).

It is easy enough to say, "God is like a father." But what does that mean? Does it mean that God is like any human father? Heaven forbid! There are many who bear the name "father" who are far from Godlike. Some people have actually found it difficult to think of God as Father for the very reason that the associations clustered around that term are unhappy ones, if not unwholesome. No, the fact is, if you want to know what God is like, you must take your clue from the words Jesus spoke to Philip. While Jesus was never a father in a physical sense, he possessed the fatherly qualities which quickly come to mind when you think of ideal fatherhood.

"He who has seen me," he said, "has seen the Father."

What are the fatherly qualities we see in Jesus? What are the qualities that help us to understand the nature and character of God? They are these: authority that is used with restraint, love that is never selfish, justice that is always tempered with mercy, and compassion that is blind to any difference in people.

I

It is the nature of God to exercise authority under restraint.

It is very easy for a human father to overuse his authority. A little boy was with his father at the county fair. The boy was interested in the amusement center with its exciting games and rides. The father was interested in the exhibits. It wasn't much fun for the youngster, being dragged along to see the things that appealed to adults, and he couldn't help showing it. At last, in exasperation, his father said, "Are you going to enjoy yourself or am I going to have to make you!" Human fathers overuse their authority, but our Eternal Father never does.

How infinitely patient our Heavenly Father is! Have you ever thought what you would do about man and our world if you were God?

Here is man, this magnificent creature God made,

and what has he done? Again and again he has bathed the world with the blood of his brother. The twentieth century will go down in history as the bloodiest century we have known yet, in spite of our so-called civilization. Again and again man has enslaved his fellowman that he might profit by exploiting him and live in comfort by the sweat of another's brow. Again and again man has found a strange pleasure in grinding another human being into the earth.

If you wonder why some people in Africa don't like the white man very much, recall what happened in this country a number of years ago. A young African was a student here. He was in a public building with some friends. Becoming thirsty, he asked for a drink of water. He was told, "There's a spittoon over there. Go drink out of that!" The young African has now become an important leader in one of the new nations in Africa.

I don't know what I would do if I were God. I think I'd throw a few thunderbolts around! I have a lot of understanding for Martin Luther, who once said, "If I were our Lord God . . . and these vile people were as disobedient as they now be, I would knock the world in pieces." I don't know how he can be so patient with us.

But when I look at Jesus, I think I can understand a little bit. One day when Jesus was on his way to Jerusalem by way of Samaria, an experience occurred which gives us a flash of insight into the nature of God. It was nearing nightfall. Jesus had sent two of his disciples ahead to a village to make preparations for them for the night.

One can picture Jesus, weary from the day's journey, easing himself to the ground to rest while his friends carried out the errand. Soon they were seen coming back. They were angry. They said the people of the village wouldn't have him. Two of the disciples, in a blistering rage, said, "Lord, do you want us to bid fire come down from heaven and consume them?" The record says that Jesus "turned and rebuked them. And they went on to another village" (Luke 9:55-56). Isn't this a picture of the patience of God?

It is to be assumed that God could use his authority and power to do anything he might wish to do. He is the creator. He has final authority over all that he has made but, like a wise father, he uses that authority sparingly. Like a wise father, he gives his children "growing room." He allows us to make mistakes, for he honors the freedom he has given us. He sets limits, as any wise father would, and when we break his rules, we are broken by them and we must suffer the consequences of what we do. He is consistent. He doesn't blow hot and cold. His wisdom is available to us whenever we are ready to turn to him. Instead of using his authority to break us, he uses his love to woo us.

God is a picture of authority in restraint. We see this in Jesus, and we know this is a worthy attribute of the one who is our Father.

II

Another quality of God is love that is never selfish.

I wish we might see this more often in human fathers.

Here is a man who wants his son to follow him in the business he has created. The boy has no interest in it. He wants to pursue his own life in his own way, and he is interested in the law. But the father has built his business out of nothing. He is proud of his efforts. It would be a shame not to have his heir carry on what he has so ably built. A noble reputation has been established. The father insists. This man does not love his son! He loves himself!

Here is another man whose son is facing the draft. The boy has searched his heart and he cannot bring himself to carry a gun and be trained to kill. His father cannot think of him being a conscientious objector to war. What would people think? What would they say about him and about the family? So the father tries to persuade. He appeals to the boy not to disgrace the family. This man's motivation is not love! It is disguised selfishness.

Again, here is a man who is eminently successful and whose business affairs take almost all his time. He has no time to spend with his son. As a substitute, he showers everything upon him. He gives him ample spending money, fine clothes, a sports car. These things are nice, but the boy is lonely for companionship with his dad. His father says he loves him. "Don't I give him everything he wants?" he says. "Yes," the answer might be, "everything but love!"

We human fathers mean well but, if we are honest with ourselves, wouldn't we have to admit that too often what we do arises out of a disguised selfishness? But this is not true of God. If Jesus is anything like God, there is no selfishness in him. Jesus could have been a king, but he chose to be a servant. He might have required others to wait on him hand and foot, but he took a basin and towel and washed the feet of his disciples. He might have carried a scepter, but he chose instead to carry a cross. The full measure of his purpose was seen one day when he said, "The Son of man also came not to be served but to serve, and to give his life" (Mark 10:45). We think of these things as we remember that Jesus said to Philip, "He who has seen me has seen the Father."

"God so loved the world that he gave . . ." (John 3:16). It is the Christian belief that "God was in Christ reconciling the world to himself" (II Cor. 5:19). This means that God was so concerned about this foolish, blundering, wayward people of his that he himself entered the world "in Christ" to help us.

Can you imagine the President of the United States going to Selma, Alabama, to help with voter registration there and being willing to go to jail and to suffer the humiliation and pain of that experience, perhaps being beaten, because he loves his peoples, all of them, whether they are black or white? That is what God did on the cross. He did not hold himself aloof from his world. He did not look upon his world with mild indifference. He took the pain of the world into his own heart. He let his people spit in his face and mock him with a purple robe and a cruel crown. He carried a cross and, before he died on it, he forgave his poor misguided people for

19

what they had done to him. Why did he do this? Because he loved to the uttermost.

The noble quality of love that is never selfish is seen in Jesus, and we know without a shadow of a doubt that this describes our Heavenly Father.

III

God is one whose justice is tempered with mercy.

In the human family the justice we mete out is not always measured with mercy. I recall a scene from a novel which portrays a stern, unbending father whose daughter has made a moral mistake. He stands at the door of his house. His pride is hurt. The family reputation has been tarnished. His eyes are hard with indignation. "Go!" he screams, "Go from this house and never come back!"

This is not a picture of God. Human parents may do this to their children, but God never does. Our Father is infinitely forgiving and full of mercy to those who do wrong. Do not misunderstand. God is not indifferent to the moral behavior of his children. He is not an indulgent parent who hides his eyes or turns the other way whenever we do something wrong. There is a moral law, and he has never set it aside. He has never declared a moratorium on the consequences of sin. But you may be sure of this: God never stands at the door and screams at his wayward child, "Go! Go from this house and never come back!" God always tempers his justice with mercy.

Here again, we catch a glimpse of the fatherly nature of God through the actions and attitudes of Jesus.

Recall the experience when a woman, taken in adultery, was thrown at the feet of Jesus. She was about to be stoned. This was the law. Jesus looked at the woman and then he looked at the self-righteous, angry men. "Let him who is without sin among you be the first to throw a stone at her," he said. There was an embarrassed silence which was broken at last only by the sound of stones dropping to the ground. Soon, only the woman and Jesus were left there. He said to her, "Woman, where are they? Has no one condemned you?" As the woman looked up at him he continued, "Neither do I condemn you; go, and do not sin again" (John 8:2-11). Sinning humanity falls at the feet of God, the Father. The consequences of sin cannot be remitted, but in the face of God man will always see forgiveness. As Jesus shows us, our Father tempers justice with mercy.

One of the great stories of the Bible is the parable of the prodigal son. This really ought to be called the parable of the loving father. We don't need anything to remind us of the depths of our sinful nature. We can read about that in our morning newspaper and find it described in all its morbid details in the latest best-selling novel. Our swine-pen life is evident everywhere. We know that prodigal—we can identify with him.

But what we need to be reminded of is the picture of the loving father. The father in Jesus' story cannot forget his cocksure, pleasure-mad son. He takes his vigil at the door every day hoping that his son will return. One day, he does return, gaunt with hunger and marred by sin. The father sees him coming and runs to meet him and throws his arms about him in his filth and rags. He kisses him and calls for the best robe in the house to be placed on his shoulders and a ring for his hand and shoes for his feet. He celebrates the return of his wayward son with a great feast (Luke 15: 11-24).

This is a picture of a loving, merciful father who understands the awfulness of sin but never stops loving the sinner. God's judgment lies in the inescapable consequences of sin. His mercy lies in his willingness to forgive.

IV

God is a loving Father whose concern and compassion are blind to any difference in people.

In the human family, sometimes we find one parent or the other, sometimes both, being partial to one of their children. This is always a devastating thing to the personality of the child who is the object of such discrimination. Here is a fine boy. It seems there isn't a serious bone in his body. Sometimes he gets into trouble. He doesn't do very well at school. He has an older brother who is a model of behavior. He is serious-minded, obedient, dependable, and he works hard at school. In the eyes of others he is pretty stuffy, but in the eyes of his parents he is very nearly perfect. The parents make unfavorable comparisons. The older boy is their "favorite" and they show it. The younger son bears the mark of his rejection as long as he lives.

Parents sometimes make this mistake, but God never does. "God shows no partiality," says Paul (Rom. 2:11). Our Father loves all his children. He is not impressed with our petty distinctions. Jesus said, "He makes his sun rise on the evil and on the good, and sends rain on the just and on the unjust" (Matt. 5:45).

Jesus shows us what God is like. He loved all the people, even those who misused him. Others could feel quite self-righteous in discriminating against the Samaritans, but Jesus demonstrated his interest in them by making a Samaritan the hero of one of his choicest stories. And who can forget the moment when Jesus offered living water to the Samaritan woman at the well? He gave himself equally to the high and to the low, to the saint and to the sinner, to the Jew and to the Samaritan. One of the bitterest criticisms against him was that he associated with social and moral outcasts. Jesus saw every person as precious in the eyes of God.

A rabbi in a Texas city was noted for his humanitarian interests. He was the inspiration of many. He would answer the call of need at any hour of the day or night whether the person was Catholic, Protestant, Jew, or nothing at all. This was often the source of amazement to less big-minded and open-hearted people. One day word came to him that a certain man was being unjustly held in jail. He went to see him and became convinced an injustice was being done. He went from one authority to another to secure the man's release but was frustrated in his efforts until he reached the top authority. After hearing his story, the official said, "Rabbi, don't you know this man is not a Jew? He is a Roman Catholic." "I know," replied the rabbi. "Why then do you go to all this trouble to help him?" countered the official. "He's a human being, isn't he?" was the simple answer. This is the way Jesus felt about all people. He saw them all as God's children.

Our Father is blind to color, national origin, and differences of language and dress. He is blind to social status and economic position. Our Father loves all his children. He has no favorites. They are all precious in his sight.

"Show us the Father, and we shall be satisfied," Philip said. And Jesus replied, "He who has seen me has seen the Father." He who has seen Jesus has seen authority that is used with restraint, love that is never selfish, justice that is tempered with mercy, and concern that is utterly blind to any difference in people.

All Men
Are Brothers

You are all brethren.

—Matt. 23:8

It is easy to overlook the obvious. A great deal of life is like looking for your glasses when you have them on. So it is with the implication of our belief in the fatherly nature of God. Jesus said, "You are all brethren . . . for you have one Father, who is in heaven." The logic of this is inescapable. There is one Father who is the Father of us all. If God is the Father of us all, then humanity is a family. If humanity is a family, all men are brothers.

Genealogy has not been a major interest in my life. I have known a few people for whom this was not only an interest but a disease! They have pointed with pride that they are the direct descendants of Sir Francis Drake or Lord Something-or-other of the Royal Court of England. This always amuses me because it takes only a few minutes of simple mathematics to figure out that one is descended from 1,028 ancestors in a period of ten generations. And if you want to go back twenty generations, you can tally 1,020,672 ancestors! One ought to be able to find somebody famous out of all that number! Of course, you always run the chance of finding something else, too! Personally, I've been a little afraid to go into it too far.

But the meaning of this is very elementary. It means that physically we are related. Our ancestral lines link up somewhere. Trace your ancestry back to the original source and you will find that we are all descendants of the first man and woman who, in turn, were born in the womb of God's mind. "You are all brethren," said Jesus, "for you have one Father, who is in heaven."

The brotherhood that Jesus proclaimed, however, is more than a matter of biology. Jesus made it a principal part of his teachings. Once when a messenger came with word that his mother and brothers were waiting for him outside, Jesus used the incident to declare dramatically, encompassing the scene before him, "Here are my mother and my brothers!" (Matt. 12:49). In the final scene of John Masefield's play The Trial of Jesus, Jesus appears and says:

> Open your heart, open your mind,
> If ye bind your souls it is me ye bind;

Ask of me: seek: and ye shall find;
Knock, and behold, the door shall yield.
O brothers, I make the world one kin;
Open your hearts and let me in,
That the reign of my Father may begin.

"You are all brethren . . . for you have one Father, who is in heaven." What about this truth that Jesus proclaimed?

I

We may as well begin with the painful fact that we haven't done too well with it.

It was one of those days when everything had gone wrong. Dad had had a hard day at his office. Mother had been hounded by people at the door and by a rash of telephone calls, so that one irritation after another had piled up into a mountain of exasperation. John had had a fight with his girl the night before and he was in a low mood. Judy had flunked an important exam. Dinner was a gloomy hour! Everyone was nursing his own private problem. It was inevitable that an explosion would occur. Cruel words were coming out. Voices were rising to a crescendo. Emotions were running high. Suddenly Judy cried out, "What's the matter with us? We're not a family!"

When we look at our human situation, we would have to say the same thing. We're not a family. We are killing each other in Viet Nam. We won't even talk with our Chinese brothers in Communist China except through

27

a neutral government. Half our human family goes to bed hungry every night, while some of us have so much food we have to diet to keep down our weight. Our Negro brothers and sisters want the same rights we white people enjoy, but it is necessary to pass a law to secure for them the rights that are already guaranteed them in the United States Constitution. Political factions within our society become so emotional that they can't talk calmly with one another. Fear makes them hate. We spread half-truths and sometimes downright lies about one another. In some parts of our world we practice what amounts to economic slavery. We used to do it in this country until we passed laws covering labor-management relations, unemployment compensation, and social security. And still there are pockets of economic servitude in this enlightened land—so much so that our government must engage in an antipoverty program in this, the richest nation of the world.

What's the matter with us? We're not a family! We have one God who is our Father. God created us all. We belong to him. Jesus calls us to recognize and live in a brotherhood relationship. Sometimes we have been able to do this when our brother looks like us, thinks like us, acts like us; but beyond that we have failed dismally.

This brings us to a question we need to ask.

II

Why have we failed to live like the family we are? For one thing, our lack of knowledge of each other has made us timid. My wife and I were on a train going from Lucerne, Switzerland, into northern Italy. We shared a compartment with a young Swiss couple. Knowing there might be language problems, we waited quite a while before we attempted conversation with the young people. We would glance at them and they at us. We would smile and they would smile. Finally, I broke the ice with an attempt at communication. The man responded with broken English and his wife responded with a warm smile. We had a wonderful visit together in spite of the language barrier, and when they left the train later we had a very happy feeling about these friends. I have thought of them many times since, wondering where they are, what they are doing; and always I think of them with warm affection.

Have you noticed how difficult it is to start a conversation with a stranger? A man sat beside me on an airplane. I glanced at him furtively to see what he was like. His face was drawn into a near-scowl. Apparently he was thinking of something not too pleasant. I sat in silence beside him for a long time, each of us lost in his own thoughts. Finally, I screwed up enough courage to speak to him and to offer him my name and my hand in friendship. When I did, he smiled, and I saw that he was very pleasant. We began to visit. I found that he was from Tucson. I asked him where he had lived before coming to the West, and to my amazement, I found he had come from southern Indiana, not more than twenty miles from the place of my birth! When we parted at the

29

airport of a city a thousand miles away, we were warm friends.

Certainly, one of the reasons why we have failed to live like the family we are intended to be is that we have lacked knowledge of one another, and this has made us afraid.

Again, why have we failed to live as a family of God? Surely, it is because it has been easier to talk brotherhood than it has been to live it. One of the best ways to get rid of a good idea is to make of it what Lincoln called a "pernicious abstraction." Thus, instead of becoming a reality, it ends up being a nice sentiment. We have talked about brotherhood for a long time. Perhaps we have talked about it so much we have become immune to it. As long as we can keep our discussion general, there is no problem; but when we begin to get specific—when we get down to individual cases—that's another matter.

Professor Bliss Perry used to tell about a dog he had when he was a boy. The dog, being very normal, chased cats. Perry noticed, however, that if the cat refused to run and turned to face the dog, the dog suddenly discovered that he had business elsewhere or that he had a flea to be scratched. Dr. Perry made the observation that cats were to be chased but not to be caught. If the cat insisted on being caught, the dog was embarrassed. So it has been with some of our great ideals. We have given chase to them, but if a big idea like brotherhood insists on being caught, we become embarrassed. Witness the Supreme Court's desegregation decision and directive. The country has been embarrassed ever since. Witness The Methodist Church's efforts to rid itself of the segregated Central Jurisdiction. It has been very embarrassing to find that our glowing words about brotherhood in race relations are so hard to get translated into reality even within the body of a church! For too long we have substituted talk for action. For too long we have hidden behind the skirts of Lincoln's "pernicious abstraction."

So! We have been afraid to involve ourselves in a deeper humanity, and we have taken refuge in fine talk which has been a substitute for the real thing.

III

Now we come to the crucial question: How can we do better?

For one thing, we need to get acquainted with people who are different from us racially, religiously, nationally, and culturally. My wife and I do a lot of traveling about the world, and we like to take people with us. There is a reason for this. We want to help build bridges of understanding and relationship between peoples of the world. We believe that when people get to know each other across all the man-made barriers we have created, they will become friends and will come to recognize their oneness of humanity.

I think the student exchange program is a big help in building good relations between people of various nations. Our work camp programs, wherein a selected

31

group of young people live and work together in some other country for a period of time or live and work among the interracial groups of the blighted areas of our great cities—these are great programs of brotherhood building. You cannot work with and live with people of another culture without feeling the deeper ties of humanity binding you into fellowship.

In a university setting, the "host family" program is a great aid to building brotherhood. We have the good fortune to have two students from other lands assigned to us. One is a student from East Pakistan. His religion is Islam. We attended a meeting not long ago at the university where his religion was explained to us. His skin is dark. The other student is from Nigeria. His religion is Anglican. His skin is ebony black. We have had these students in our home frequently. We have learned about their families, their customs and traditions, their hopes and dreams. We have come to love them. Thus is the spirit of brotherhood built.

We have something going for us in the increasing interdependence of man as our planet is made smaller and smaller with each technological advance. Dr. Arthur Compton, the eminent physicist, commented on this some time ago. Writing in *Saturday Review*, he said, "We see ourselves living increasingly in the lives of each other." He recalled the thesis of William James that the self is much more than a man's skin—that it includes everything about that person, even his family and friends. Then Dr. Compton said, "What technology is doing is to extend this 'selfhood' to include an ever-widening circle. It includes, to a greater or lesser degree, all of mankind."

"Getting to know you" is more than a song to sing. It is an experience that must be universalized if we are to make brotherhood real upon the earth.

For another thing, if we are to do better in realizing the brotherhood Jesus proclaimed, we must strengthen every agency that makes for human understanding and builds healthy human relationships. The United Nations is such an agency. Granted that it has its problems. Granted that it has severe limitations. Still, it has been a useful forum for airing national differences; and its nonpolitical activities alone, contributing to world cooperation and understanding, are enough to justify its existence. Through the UN Special Fund, the International Development Association, the World Bank, and the regional commissions, the United Nations has contributed much to economic and technological progress. Secretary of State Dean Rusk, in his Dag Hammarskjöld memorial lecture at Columbia University, said, "Anyone who questions the need for international technical organizations like the United Nations Agencies dealing with maritime matters, civil aviation, telecommunications, atomic energy, and meteorology simply does not recognize the times in which we live." Who can measure the humanitarian value of the World Health Organization in raising global health standards, UNESCO in reducing illiteracy, and the Food and Agriculture Organization in increasing food production in many underdeveloped countries?

The missionary program of the church is another agency that must be encouraged and strengthened. World travelers tell us that the greatest cells of good will in the world are to be found where the church has gone to lift men and women to a better life by healing their sick, educating their children, and training their people in better methods of agriculture and animal husbandry. The Methodist program of short-term missionaries is especially commendable. Through this program outstanding young men and women who have completed college are sent to a mission field for a three-year period to work among the people. The United States Government paid this idea a great compliment when it established the Peace Corps. Much of the Peace Corps' structure and method were patterned after this short-term missionary program.

The work of the World Council of Churches, the Vatican Council, and all such ecumenical programs must be supported. All these are helping us to realize that all men are brothers and that we have one Father who is the Father of us all. We need to strengthen every agency that works toward this end.

What else can we do to implement our Lord's dreams of brotherhood? It will help if we begin calling any violation of our brotherhood relationship by its right name—sin! As a parish minister, I have had many people come to my study to confess a sin. In deepest confidence and often with heartbreaking sobs they have poured out their story of misconduct in sex, business, family, or social relations. But I have yet to have someone seek me out and say, "Pastor, I have sinned. I have sinned terribly. I have participated in a real estate conspiracy to deny housing to Negroes in a certain part of town." Or, "Pastor, I have sinned. I declined to employ a Jew, not because he wasn't competent but because he was a Jew." Or, "Pastor, I have sinned. A neighbor of mine is a Mexican, and I had a neighborhood gathering at my house and didn't invite her just because she was a Mexican."

If the family relationship Jesus talked about is to be realized, the time must come when the practice of discrimination because of race, creed, or national origin will be regarded as a sin fully as evil as lying, cheating, stealing, adultery, or murder.

One thing more we must do. We must be willing to build our piece of the trail of brotherhood to the summit of achievement even though we may never be permitted to reach the summit ourselves.

There was a group of young mountain climbers who set out to scale a mountain which had never before been conquered. After a long period of preparation and much publicity, they began their high adventure. From the valley below the people watched through their binoculars. Sometimes the adventurous company was in view and sometimes not. At last they disappeared from view altogether. A long time afterward someone reported that the party had returned to the village and that they had been defeated in their exploit. A reporter went to interview them. They were weary to the point of exhaustion. "Were you not terribly disappointed?"

35

the reporter asked. The leader of the group responded for them all. He said, "No. You see, mountains are climbed on the shoulders of other men. A part of the way we went up along the line that other climbers had gone. Then, we came to the place where no man had ever gone, and for some distance after that we blazed the trail. We reached our limit, but someday some other men will follow us, go safely over the advanced route we have traveled, and carry on. Perhaps sometime—no one knows when—someone will reach the summit, but at least a part of the way he travels will be the way we have marked for him."

Man has conquered many frontiers. He has conquered the sea and the wilderness. He has conquered the frozen wastes of the North and South Poles. He has conquered the mightiest mountain of them all, Mt. Everest. He has conquered the atom. He has conquered the sky, and is well on the way to conquering outer space. But there is one frontier that he has neglected to the peril of his soul, and perhaps even to the peril of his existence on this planet. That is the frontier of brotherhood.

Jesus of Nazareth blazed the trail for us when he said, "You are all brethren," and when he lived the life of brotherhood among us. It remains for us to follow that trail resolutely toward the summit!

People
Have Value

You are of more value than many sparrows.
—Luke 12:7

The dignity and worth of persons were made perfectly clear by Jesus.

Our Lord was in conflict with the Pharisees over several things, but none was more important than their attitude toward persons. One day Jesus invited a despised tax collector to be his disciple. Later he went to his home where a dinner was served, and he mingled freely with other tax collectors. For the Pharisees, it was a scandal to associate with such people. For Jesus, this was his mission. In the eyes of the Pharisees, these people were worthless. In the eyes of Jesus, they were worthy of God's redeeming love. He said, "I came not to call the righteous, but sinners" (Mark 2:17).

At another time, Jesus' disciples were going through some grain fields on the sabbath day. They were hungry. They plucked some of the grain and ate it. The Pharisees condemned them for "working" on the sabbath day. Jesus defended them. As far as he was concerned, their hunger was more important than religious rules.

More than once Jesus healed people on the sabbath day. He was condemned for this, for it was contrary to the law. But always the need of people transcended religious restrictions. The reason? People have value in the eyes of God, and Jesus reflected this in what he said and did.

The Jews despised the Samaritans and would have nothing to do with them, but Jesus offered living water to one of them. To him, they were not Samaritans—they were people. He saw them as having the same value as God's chosen people. They were just as worthy of salvation as the high priest himself!

In an adult world, children are often overlooked as though they don't count for much. But this was not the way Jesus regarded children. When the disciples tried to keep people from bringing the children to him, he rebuked his friends and said, "Let the children come to me, and do not hinder them; for to such belongs the kingdom of heaven" (Matt. 19:14). And, on another occasion he said, "Whoever causes one of these little ones . . . to sin, it would be better for him to have a great millstone fastened round his neck and to be drowned in the depths of the sea" (Matt. 18:6). What Jesus was saying is that children are people, and people have value. They are precious in the eyes of God. They must be treated in the manner in which God regards them.

Jesus believed people to be so valuable in the sight of God that the most minute matters, even to the hairs of a man's head, are of concern to him. Jesus spoke of sparrows. He said you could buy five of them for two pennies but not one of them is forgotten before God. Then he said, "Fear not; you are of more value than many sparrows."

Yes, Jesus clearly proclaimed the sacredness and worth of human personality. This has exceedingly important implications.

I

Looking back, we can see that Jesus' estimate of human life has brought about some important changes in man's history.

It has made a difference in the status of women. Here in America women and men are treated as equals. But this has not always been so. In some parts of the world women are still treated as chattel. Wherever Christianity has gone, it has made a difference in the treatment of women because of its emphasis on the value of human personality.

Institutions of healing have come from this ethical

39

concern for persons. One of the major services of the missionary impulse has been the establishment of hospitals and the sending of missionary doctors. Dr. Schweitzer's hospital at Lambaréné is perhaps the best known, but there are medical centers on all mission fields.

Centers of learning have developed from this same concern for persons. Wherever Christianity has gone, schools have been opened and colleges and universities have been established. The first college in America was started by the church.

Recently I had occasion to talk with Dr. Frank C. Laubach. He has taken his literacy program to 103 countries of the world. Why has he done this? He knows that people cannot better themselves without knowledge. To gain knowledge, they must learn to read. He sees people in terms of their dignity and worth. To help them to read enhances their worth and their ability to lift themselves to new levels of living. Frank Laubach learned this from One who believed profoundly in the value of persons.

Prison reform has come from the application of this principle of the worth of people. In state after state capital punishment has been abolished. More and more the rehabilitation of criminals is assuming greater importance than their punishment.

The shameful practice of slavery was brought to an end because of this Christian humanitarian concern. Twenty miles off the coast of Africa in the Indian Ocean is the island of Zanzibar. During the slave-trading days, natives were brought from the interior of Africa and sold as slaves on the island of Zanzibar. A visitor to that island today will find an interesting thing. On the site of the old slave market now stands an Anglican church. There is a worthy symbolism in that. A cruel institution such as slavery cannot stand before the ethical onslaught of the Christian gospel. Over a hundred years ago Christian missionaries, exploring and penetrating into the interior of Africa, helped to abolish this shameful practice.

One thinks of Lord Shaftesbury in England. In Shaftesbury's time children were made to work in the coal mines, deep in the bowels of the earth. They were very useful, for they could go into spaces too small for a man to enter. Children in those days worked fourteen and fifteen hours a day in the mines, some of them never seeing the light of day. Shaftesbury, with his humanitarian concern which he caught from Jesus, took up the battle for the rights of children. And the day came when child labor laws were enacted to abolish that evil.

You see, Christianity is a humanitarian religion. It has endeavored to elevate people to a new dignity. And the reason for this is that Jesus of Nazareth believed so profoundly in the sacred worth of persons.

II

Because of the truth of what Jesus proclaimed, man's quest for freedom is given encouragement and hope.

41

This has been called the age of rising expectations. The oppressed people of the world—the backward people—are coming into their own. New nations are being born with such rapidity that the map makers can hardly keep up with the changes. If you haven't bought a new map of the world within the last six months, what you have is out of date. Recently I read a book on Africa which was written just last year. The author very wisely indicated in the foreword that there would doubtless be political changes in Africa before the book could be published. She was right.

Wallace Hamilton has a book under the interesting title *The Thunder of Bare Feet*. He speaks of "the many, rising up to be the rulers. The shirtless millions . . . climbing up to power. The barefoot ones . . . walking up the steps into the palace." This is happening in Africa and Asia. Anyone who has ears to hear can perceive the "thunder of bare feet."

Well, Christianity encourages this. The gospel of Jesus proclaims that no man shall be ground under the heel of another. It proclaims that every man is important to God regardless of his color, his national origin, or any other distinction. The great movements for freedom can and should take encouragement and hope from the Christian affirmation of the worth of persons.

Our country was conceived in the womb of freedom. I like to think of the beginnings of this land of ours. Our forefathers came to these shores that they might have religious freedom. The war of the revolution was fought in order that we might be able to govern ourselves. Whenever I see the Statue of Liberty in New York Harbor, my heart is quickened with the thought that so many people have come to America to find freedom. I recall the words of Emma Lazarus inscribed at the base of the statue:

> Give me your tired, your poor,
> Your huddled masses yearning to breathe free,
> The wretched refuse of your teeming shore,
> Send these, the homeless, tempest-tost to me,
> I lift my lamp beside the golden door.

We are proud of that. But we have not always remem-bered that we are a land of the free. We have some un-fortunate chapters in our history. The era of McCarthy-ism is one of them. Our treatment of the minorities is far from a proud chapter in our history. White Anglo-Saxon Protestants have demanded liberty for themselves but have not always given it to others. In all this we have forgotten what our Lord declared about the worth of persons.

But we have had our noble moments too. An in-teresting experience occurred at the University of Cal-ifornia at Los Angeles a few years ago. A commencement speaker had been engaged who did not meet the approval of a relatively small but demonstrative polit-ical group of students and townspeople. On the day of the graduation exercises, a picket line was formed and began to march near the entrance to the campus. Placards proclaimed the nature of the complaint in blatant and dramatic ways. The incident began to attract large crowds of curious spectators. I was attracted too. I observed the police captain moving in and out of the throng keeping an eye on the picket line. Knowing him slightly, I made my way to him and greeted him saying, "What's going on here, captain?" His face broke into a broad smile, and with obvious pride in his voice he said, "This is America!"

Here is where we have our quarrel with fascist and communist governments. Recall the fascist states ruled by Hitler and Mussolini. In those lands the state was supreme and the individual was nothing. In the communist governments of Cuba, Red China, Soviet Russia, and East Germany, the rights of the individual are secondary to the dictates of the state. Communism speaks of the dictatorship of the proletariat as though the people constitute a sacred value. But actually, if any individual has the misfortune of getting in the way of the accomplishment of the aims of the state, it is disastrous for him. The individual is dispensable. This is not right. It is contrary to Jesus' conviction that every person has value.

As long as man breathes, as long as he quests for dignity and freedom and personal worth, he can take encouragement and hope from what Jesus proclaimed about persons. People have value.

III

This conviction of Jesus should cause us individually to search our hearts and practices.

Parents must be willing to apply this test to their relationships with their children. I know how trying children can be. I used to live in a neighborhood where there were a number of them. Our front yard often became the playground for the children living on either side of us. One day I was studying at home. It was warm, and the window was open. I could hear the children at play out in the yard. They had tired of one game and were about to begin another. I overheard one little girl say, "I want to be half human and half monster." Then I heard a little boy say, "I want to be all monster!" Well, sometimes our children seem like little monsters! But how do we treat them? Do we treat them as lamentable inconveniences or as priceless values?

An Oregon rancher wanted to send his young son to Montana. The boy was too small to travel alone. The rancher went into town and made his way to the post office. When the postmaster came to the window, the rancher shuffled his feet in embarrassment and said, "I wanted to ask if there is any way to send my boy to Montana by parcel post." The postmaster ran his hand over his stubbly beard and replied, "I don't know—I'll look it up." He went back among his regulation books in search of an answer to the question. Then he returned to the window and said, "I guess it's all right. I don't find anything that says you can't. But," he continued, "I'll have to ask you a question. What valuation would you place on the boy?" There was a twinkle in his eye as he said it, and the rancher caught the full implication

45

of it. His face broke into a broad grin and he said, "I wouldn't know how to do that!"

Young people must be willing to test their relationships with one another by asking, "How do I treat my date—as something to be exploited for a cheap thrill or as a person whose worth is highest in the scale of values?" There is something of a heavenly inspiration in the way in which young lovers look at each other. It is a mixture of longing and worship. This is as it should be. Even the endearments used by a couple in love express the very point we are making. Each one is "precious" to the other.

This attitude should not cease with marriage. Husbands and wives should periodically examine themselves to prevent any spirit of selfish regard from creeping into their relationship. What a wonderful thing it is when, after a half century of life together, one can say as an octogenarian said of his wife, "Whenever Mary enters the room where I am—even if I don't see her—my heart glows within me!" Whether one may have this exalted kind of love or not, every husband and wife needs to ask, "How do we treat each other—as property or as persons of worth and dignity?"

We must be willing to apply the principle of person-value to what we say about people. It is so easy to pass on as true what has come to us as unverified gossip about someone. We don't mean to do any harm, but words can be very cruel and they are impossible to recall. Will Carleton has written:

46

Boys flying kites haul in their white-winged birds,
You can't do that when you're flying words.
Careful with fire is good advice, we know;
Careful with words is ten times doubly so.
Thoughts unexpressed sometimes fall back dead,
But God himself can't kill them when they're said.

Let the employer examine his attitude toward his workmen. Are they regarded as tools to be used without respect for their feelings and their well-being, or are they to be viewed as persons of individual worth? Let the teacher search his own mind to see how he looks upon his students. The story is told about a certain headmaster that whenever he went before his class of boys he would bow to them before beginning his lecture. It was his way of showing his respect for the persons he was privileged to teach. He recognized their worth. He saw his job of teaching as that of helping personalities to unfold into their highest possibilities. Let the merchant ask himself, "How do I think of my customers—as persons to be exploited or as individuals to be served?" There are certain kinds of businesses, even though they are legitimate, which cannot stand this test. One of these is the liquor business. I have yet to see a dignified drunk man or woman. We are all under obligation, no matter who we are or what business we engage in, to examine ourselves in relation to others and to ask, "What effect does my work have on people— does it elevate them or does it degrade them?"

Anyone can complete this process of personal application. The next time you get a chance, go to your mirror and stand there looking at yourself. Look deeply into your eyes. Then say, "I am a child of God. I am important to my Heavenly Father. Among all that God created I have a special place that is only a little lower than the angels." This will make your head come erect. You will square your shoulders. You will stand tall. Your face will relax in a smile. Then look at yourself once more and say with measured words, "This is true not only of myself—it is true of my mate. It is true of my children. It is true of my neighbors. It is true of every person in my town. It is true of every person on the face of the earth. People have value, and I shall treat them that way."

It is interesting to reflect upon the value of the human body. Years ago I came across a chemical analysis of the human body. At that time the market value of all these components came to about $1.98. Recently I read of a new kind of value analysis. This time, the body was studied in terms of its atomic energy potential. This was broken down into kilowatt hours of power. On this basis, it was estimated that a 150-pound man was worth 85½ billion dollars! This is getting closer to the truth. When Jesus referred to the sparrows and said, "Not one of them is forgotten before God . . . and you are of more value than many sparrows," he was not rendering a chemical or atomic estimate of man. He was saying the value that is given to people is infinite and immeasurable!

Character
Is Primary

The gate is narrow and the way is hard, that leads to life.

—Matt. 7:14

Among the truths Jesus proclaimed, an important place must be given to the idea that character is basic. The Master emphasized it repeatedly in his teachings. His calls to repentance reflect his conviction that character changes are fundamental. He condemned the scribes and Pharisees for their hypocrisy and for their lack of concern to keep the inside of the cup as clean as the outside. He explained to his disciples that what comes from the heart is important. If it is evil, a man is defiled. "Out of the heart come evil thoughts, murder, adultery, fornication, theft, false witness, slander." (Matt. 15:19.) Scathing was the Master's denunciation of certain scribes who paraded their religion, but devoured widows' houses.

When Jesus was instructing the twelve disciples, he made crystal clear how important it was for them to be morally sound. In dramatic and symbolic language he said it would be better to sacrifice a hand or a foot or an eye than for them to be morally and spiritually maimed. No price, he was saying, is too great to pay for character. "What can a man give in return for his life?" (Mark 8:37.) "The gate is narrow and the way is hard, that leads to life," but the alternative is the way to destruction.

But more than anything Jesus said about character being of prime importance, he underscored this truth with his life. Recall his experience in the wilderness following his baptism, when he was charting the course of his life. He was aware of a strange and wonderful power surging through him. The temptation came to him to use this power selfishly—for his own physical satisfactions. He discarded this as an unworthy thing to do. He was tempted to gain success by spectacular means. This, too, he dismissed. Then he was tempted to use this power of which he was freshly aware to gain control of the world. He would not permit such a thought to remain in his mind. This experience of Jesus spells out in unmistakable language that which he came to proclaim. Character comes first. It is basic. Personal success and power perhaps are to be desired, but character comes first. Jesus was saying to himself, "Alluring as these things are, I turn aside from them.

More than anything else I must be true to the best that is in me."

Jesus faced all this again on the night of his betrayal. He could have slipped away from his enemies that night. He could have withdrawn in safety to another part of the little country. By being careful he could have lived to a ripe old age. But he chose instead to face the dangerous alternative of the cross. He didn't say it with his lips, but he said it with his life, "It is better to die than to betray yourself. Deny what is deep within you, and though you have everything, you have nothing."

I

Character is primary within the inner life of a person.

Man was made to be moral, and when he tries to live in any other way, he goes to pieces. A churchman of international reputation was telling of a college friend. He was a lean, ascetic youth with fire in his eye—the kind of idealist who was out of patience with anyone who accepted things as they are. The churchman said, "We were ridiculous young prigs, but we did have our dream, and my friend had a better dream than mine." They completed their college course and went their separate ways. The young idealist with fire in his eye became a journalist, and for some time he was a foreign correspondent for a British journal. Now and then news would trickle back from Paris, St. Petersburg, Constantinople, Berlin, and elsewhere. The years went by, and one day these two men were to meet again. The

51

churchman learned that his old college friend was in the same city where he had an engagement. He took occasion to visit him. When he saw him, he said, "I did not at first recognize him. The lean, austere youth had become a sleek, well-groomed man of the world. The ascetic, wistful face was fleshy and hard; the eyes were dead. And when I recalled our youthful enthusiasms, he sneered. I am not sitting in judgment on him. I do not know what temptation overtook him. I cannot tell by what stratagem his soul had been taken. But as I left I knew that I had seen a murdered soul." To disregard the moral requirements of one's life is to engage in the murder of self.

One might almost say that the chief purpose of Jesus' life was to minister to murdered souls. He said concerning himself, "The Son of man came to seek and to save the lost" (Luke 19:10). There was Nicodemus, who was murdering his soul with a meaningless religious respectability. To him Jesus said, "You must be born anew" (John 3:7). You must start all over! There was the woman at the well who was murdering her soul with sex. She had had a number of husbands, and the man she was then living with was not her husband. To her, Jesus offered water to drink that would quench her thirsting forever. There was a young man of wealth, who was murdering his soul with self-centeredness. He was surrounded with all the comforts of life, and yet he was dissatisfied. To him Jesus said, "Go, sell what you possess and give to the poor, . . . and come, follow me" (Matt. 19:21). Jesus knew that character meant life. Without it, one might exist for a time in a physical sort of way, but the essential thing inside would be dead.

Cyrano de Bergerac knew this. A friend was trying to persuade him to accept a retainer's fee so that he could write his poetry without concern for making a living. "What would you have me do?" said Cyrano.

> Seek for the patronage of some great man,
> And like a creeping vine on a tall tree
> Crawl upward, where I cannot stand alone?
> No, thank you! Dedicate, as others do,
> Poems to pawnbrokers? Be a buffoon
> In the vile hope of teasing out a smile
> On some cold face? No, thank you! Eat a toad
> For breakfast every morning? Make my knees
> Callous, and cultivate a supple spine,—
> Wear out my belly groveling in the dust?
> No, thank you! Scratch the back of any swine
> That roots up gold for me? Tickle the horns
> Of Mammon with my left hand, while my right,
> Too proud to know his partner's business,
> Takes in the fee? No, thank you! Use the fire
> God gave me to burn incense all day long
> Under the nose of wood and stone? No, thank you!
> Shall I . . . struggle to insinuate my name
> Into the columns of the Mercury?
> No, thank you! Calculate, scheme, be afraid,
> Love more to make a visit than a poem,
> Seek introductions, favors, influences?—
> No, thank you. No, I thank you! And again
> I thank you! But . . .

To sing, to laugh, to dream,
To walk in my own way, and be alone,
Free, with an eye to see things as they are,
A voice that means manhood—to cock my hat
Where I choose—At a word, a Yes, a No,
To fight—or write. To travel any road
Under the sun, under the stars, nor doubt
If fame or fortune lie beyond the bourne—
Never to make a line I have not heard
In my own heart; yet with all modesty
To say: "My soul, be satisfied with flowers,
With fruit, with weeds even; but gather them
In one garden you may call your own."
So, when I win some triumph, by some chance,
Render no share to Caesar—in a word,
I am too proud to be a parasite,
And if my nature lacks the germ that grows
Towering to heaven like the mountain pine,
Or like the oak, sheltering multitudes—
I stand, not high it may be—but alone!

My soul stands up and cheers a man like that! Yes, moral integrity is primary within the inner life.

II

It is exceedingly important also in one's personal relationship with others.

Can anyone imagine the close personal relationships of our existence holding together very long without the ingredient of moral integrity? Here are two men in conversation. They have something they want to do together. They make a date. One of them says, "I'll meet you at ten o'clock," and names the place. The other agrees. The point is this: Not even as simple a matter as an appointment could take place with any degree of dependability without the integrity that goes with character! Here is a young couple. They find a certain fulfillment of life in each other. One day they stand before a minister and each one says to the other, "From this day forward, for better, for worse, for richer, for poorer, in sickness and in health, to love and to cherish, till death us do part." It is a sacred moment for the lovers. Afterward, the minister delivers to them a piece of paper on which their marriage is recorded. But when we ponder this matter, we realize that the marriage license is not worth the paper it is written on without the element of moral integrity in the man and the woman. One wonders what this means when one out of three marriages today comes to a tragic end in the divorce courts! Here are two men who plan a business venture together. They gather up all their financial resources and combine them. Carefully they make their plans, determining what each is to do and how they will proceed. Perhaps they will draw up some legal papers spelling out what their relationship and responsibilities will be. Whether they do this or not, we realize that their partnership will fail completely without an intangible factor we call character! I do not know a single personal relationship into which the element of moral dependability does not enter. Jesus was right in proclaiming both by word and example that character is primary.

There is a strong section in the Sermon on the Mount which easily can be misunderstood. In it, Jesus points out some of the ancient legalisms and then goes far beyond them. After each one of these negative injunctions, Jesus continues, "But I say . . ." and points out another dimension of conduct which, if taken literally, would require superhuman powers. You shouldn't even be angry. You mustn't have a lustful thought. You shouldn't use an oath at all. You should always render good for evil, even to turning the other cheek when someone strikes you. You should love your enemies. This we need to remember—Jesus was not setting up an impossible standard of conduct. It was not his intention to substitute a new legalism for an old one. Jesus did not deal in negatives, but in positives. What Jesus was doing here was placing dramatic emphasis upon the fact that the key to conduct in interpersonal relations is a strong sense of rightness and wrongness—an inner core of character—that determines right relations with people over and above any law that requires it.

During the last war, a flyer was returning to his base after a dangerous mission. His plane had been damaged by enemy fire, and he was bringing it in on "a wing and a prayer." It became evident that he could not make it back to his field. One engine was dead and the other was faltering. He radioed the field that he was going to try an emergency landing. Since it was almost certain suicide to attempt a forced landing in that area, the pilot was instructed to bail out and forsake the plane.

In crisp tones, the pilot replied, "I can't do that!" "Why not?" snapped the officer at the field base. "My navigator is badly wounded, and I can't move him," was the terse reply. Miraculously, a small open area appeared; and the pilot skillfully executed a crash landing from which he emerged with injuries, but with his life and that of his navigator.

There is something of the heroic that sleeps in every man's breast. It is firmly rooted in the soil of character. And it is this same factor which—in less spectacular ways—operates in day-to-day interpersonal relations. It takes only a little thought to realize that the quality of our personal relations with others is determined by the degree of moral dependability we possess.

III

Not only is character primary within the inner life of a person and in one's personal relationships with others, but it is of infinite importance in public life. Civilization without character is impossible.

This is the point of Toynbee's monumental *Study of History.* The great historian examined twenty-one civilizations, including our own, and concluded that the chief factor in the fall of civilizations was disintegration. Cultures die from the inside—from festering deterioration. This is to say what Jesus proclaimed long ago— character is primary.

Our present civilization is threatened in the same manner. A little girl came home from school with pride over what she had learned that day. She was eager to tell someone. "Daddy," she exclaimed eagerly, "I learned what the earth does every twenty-four hours!" "What does it do, honey?" her father dutifully asked. "It revolts on its abscess!" was the reply. There is a sickness that has laid its hand upon our world. It is the same sickness that has attacked other civilizations—moral infection. It behooves us to be forever alert to the slow disease that has endangered every civilization of the past.

In this connection, we see the importance of leadership that operates from a basic level of moral responsibility. Since masses of people follow their leaders, either good or bad, it is imperative that governments be directed by men of integrity. The late Lecomte du Nouy, in his *Human Destiny*, likened the history of humanity to the picture of a climbing vine. He says, "If its prop is pulled up or broken, the plant creeps along the ground, unknowingly seeking a new support, another occasion to raise itself above the weeds, and as soon as it has found one it clings to it in an unconscious but untiring effort toward the light. It is sometimes mistaken; its choice may be bad; the branch it has adopted may be rotten; that is not its fault. The human flock obeys an obscure order: it must rise, and it cannot do so without a leader."

How important it is, therefore, that national and international leaders be men of strong character. The words of Josiah Gilbert Holland come to mind.

CHARACTER IS PRIMARY

God give us men! A time like this demands
Strong minds, great hearts, true faith, and ready hands;
Men whom the lust of office does not kill;
Men whom the spoils of office cannot buy;
Men who possess opinions and a will;
Men who have honor,—men who will not lie;
Men who can stand before a demagogue,
And damn his treacherous flatteries without winking!
Tall men, sun-crowned, who live above the fog
In public duty, and in private thinking;
For while the rabble, with their thumb-worn creeds,
Their large professions and their little deeds,—
Mingle in selfish strife, lo! Freedom weeps,
Wrong rules the land, and waiting Justice sleeps!

Never has a civilization known such a high degree of technological advance as ours. We can speak into a little device called a microphone, and our voice can be heard simultaneously around the world. But the question is: Have we anything worth saying? We can stand in front of a camera and be seen by fifty million people in America through the miracle of television. But the question is: What difference does that make? We can fly faster than the speed of sound. But the question is: Where are we going in such a hurry? We can control the mysterious atom. But the question is: To what end? Life or death? We remember the solemn words of Dr. David Bradley: "Mankind can extinguish itself, mixing science with arrogance and ignorance." With President Dickey of Dartmouth, we realize that our competence must be matched with conscience, or civilization is doomed.

But it is not alone a matter of leadership, important as that is. The man on the street—the Mr. Nobody in Everytown—has an important contribution to make to the welfare of our culture too. Moral leadership that fails to find an answering response in the hearts of people is rendered ineffective.

Here is a man who went broke on a farm in southern Indiana. He was farming bottom land, and a series of floods for three successive years was too much for his limited financial resources. He sold his few possessions at a public auction and moved to town. Industry provided him employment there. Though his heart was with the soil, he worked conscientiously at his job, making sure that he always exchanged a full day's work for a full day's pay. He was respected for his honesty. He owed no man. His word was like a bond. The church was an important part in his life, and he was always to be found in his pew on Sunday. He supported worthwhile things and exercised his citizenship responsibilities regularly at the polls. Periods of unemployment, during the depression years, brought gray to his hair and lines of worry to his face, but somehow he managed to keep body and soul together for himself and his family. He was injured at his work one day, and a long and painful convalescence shortened his years. Upon retirement he lived on a modest pension, and when he died many friends came to the church for his funeral. They wiped their eyes and said to one another, "He was such a good man!" You will not find this man's name written in the history books. He was never regarded as a leader. He was never the mayor of the town—nor was he the head of his lodge. He was merely "Mr. American," whose character was as sturdy as the rock of Gibraltar. I know, because this man was my father.

If civilization is built on the foundation of moral and ethical leadership, the foundation is laid on the solid rock of men and women of unquestionable integrity.

The daily newspaper gives us the bad news of people who have messed up their lives and the lives of others. There is something significant about this, for it is the unusual that makes news. I do not care particularly for the sensationalism we find in the press, but sustained reflection on the matter yields more comfort and encouragement than we might guess. It means that the moral health of most of our people is sound. It means that Mr. Average Man is still doing his work, is honest in his dealings, is honorable in his family life, and is settling his difficulties with others without taking the law into his own hands. When this kind of man becomes unusual enough to be "news," civilization will be dead.

Jesus was right. Character is primary in private living, in personal relations with others, and in all our social experience. It is the foundation on which the structure of human life is built. Anything less is shifting sand. Mark Twain mixed wisdom with his humor when he counseled, "So live that when you die, even the undertaker will weep at your funeral."

Service
Is Supreme

The Son of man came not to be served but to serve, and to give his life.

—Matt. 20:28

When the disciples were in an argument about greatness one day, Jesus said, "Whoever would be great among you must be your servant." He climaxed this by saying, "The son of man came not to be served but to serve, and to give his life." In other words, Jesus was saying there is no greater calling in the world than that of serving others. Service is supreme.

I

Jesus made this crystal clear by what he said and did. Two of his choicest stories were on this theme. The first of these features a Samaritan and a man who was attacked by robbers. The victim was left dying beside the road. Two churchmen came by, but neither of them stopped to assist the wounded man. However, a Samaritan, detested by the Jews, was moved by the stranger's plight and stopped to help him. He administered first aid, converted his donkey into an ambulance, and took the victim to the nearest hostel where he arranged for his care.

The point of the story was plain: Jesus was illustrating the law of love. He was saying that high office in the church and correct belief about religion is not enough. Even the lawyer who stood there with a cocked ear could see that the only thing that really matters is a spirit of loving helpfulness.

In a day when so many people seem to feel that the world owes them a living, it is refreshing to recall this story about a man who felt he owed the world a loving.

The second story Jesus told makes the same point in an even more dramatic way. This parable of the Last Judgment is the subject of Michelangelo's great fresco in the Sistine Chapel at Rome. A visitor to the Vatican will never forget Michelangelo's magnificent scene. The people are being separated by a righteous judge. Some go to the right and some to the left. The expressions on the faces painted by the great artist and the violent gestures of some are a dramatic evidence of the finality of the divine decision. And yet the decision is not based on the vindictive wrath of the judge—it is already made in the lives of the people themselves. What was the principle of the separation? It was one question only: Did you help your fellowman in need? That's all there was to it. Someone was hungry. Did you feed him? Someone was thirsty. Did you give him water? Someone was a stranger. Did you offer him your friendship? Someone was freezing from the cold. Did you put a coat about his shoulders? Someone was dying. Did you comfort him? Someone was in prison. Did you care? There is nothing in the story about whether a person subscribed to a certain creed or belonged to a certain church. The point of the story is painfully blunt. Did you help the hungry, the thirsty, the lonely, the naked, the sick, the imprisoned? If so, come and stand with the righteous! If not . . . !

As one who lives in a privileged country, I find myself strangely uncomfortable in the presence of this story. Henry Smith Leiper has done a dramatic thing. He has taken the population of the world and reduced it to a single town of one thousand people. He showed that 60 persons would represent the present population of the United States with the rest of the world being represented by 940. In such a town, he said, the 60 Americans would be receiving half the total income of the entire community; the 940 other persons would share the remaining half. The 60 Americans would possess 15½ times as much goods per person as all the rest of the people. On an average they would produce 16 percent of the town's total food supply, but would consume all but 1½ percent of that and keep most of it for their own future use in expensive storage equipment. Since most of the 940 non-Americans in the community would always be hungry and never quite know when they would get enough to eat, the situation created by this disparity of food supply and the existence of vast food reserves becomes readily apparent, particularly in view of the fact that Americans already eat 72 percent above the maximum food requirements. Of the 60 Americans the lowest income groups would be better off than the average in much of the rest of the town. I am troubled by this as I contemplate the story of the Last Judgment.

Yes, there is no question about it—Jesus believed and taught that serving one's fellowman stands at the head of the list, but Jesus did more than talk about this. He demonstrated it with his own life.

Every young man stands at a fork in the road when he is ready to begin his lifework. He is aware of the years of training and preparation that have brought him to this point. He is conscious of the special gifts and capacities with which he has been endowed. Now, he must decide how he is to use this training and these gifts. Is his primary purpose to make money, to gain power, to advance himself socially?

Fundamentally, the choice Jesus had to make at the beginning of his public ministry was the same. He sought the solitude of the desert to think it through. He knew the people were looking for a Messiah. This was the hope of generations. He sensed that he had a special role to play at this point. But the question was: As the Messiah, should he rule or should he serve?

The answer was made very plain in the temptation story. He turned aside from material comforts, sensationalism, and earthly power. He refused to be a king and chose instead to be a servant!

He returned to his home town, and when they invited him to have a part in the conduct of worship in the temple, he deliberately selected a reading from Isaiah that indicated the unwavering purpose of his life:

> The Spirit of the Lord is upon
>   me,
> because he has anointed me to
>   preach good news to the poor.
> He has sent me to proclaim release
>   to the captives
> and recovering of sight to the blind,
> to set at liberty those who are op-
>   pressed,
> to proclaim the acceptable year of
>   the Lord (Luke 4:18-19).

His entire ministry was one of service.

There is an eloquent scene in John's Gospel. It is the time of the Last Supper. The moments are pregnant with solemnity. As the disciples talk in muted tones, the Master rises from the table, secures a basin of water and a towel, and stoops to wash the feet of his followers. It is an act of lowly service. When he has finished, he says, "I have given you an example" (John 13:15).

66

Indeed, our lord has given us an unforgettable example. Who can ever erase that picture from his mind? Here is the Lord of Life himself bending low before the men who would, with but one exception, forsake him in a few hours, performing an act of menial service. Can you imagine the president of a university washing the feet of his students? Can you think of a prime minister washing the feet of the gardeners who tend his lawns?

By this example, Jesus has toppled all our little idols of greatness. By it, he has declared in vivid language that the greatest thing in the world is to serve others. The lowliest service is the highest calling of all.

His final example of this was the cross.

II

This important tenet of Jesus reflects a need in everyone to be altruistic.

Out of World War II comes an account of a group of American soldiers who were assigned to escort a shipment of heavy machinery from Okinawa to Burma. Each of them had a little money, and as they journeyed they talked of the possibility of buying silk goods and other things in Hong Kong because of the very favorable exchange rate. When they reached Hong Kong, the sight of starving children sleeping in the gutters was too much for them. They saw emaciated old people and homeless refugees, and a wave of compassion swept over them. They decided to pool their money and give it to a food fund for the hungry people. When they put it together, it totaled $680. The soldiers completed their mission and returned to their base. They were surprised to find a citation waiting for them there. Word of their generosity had been passed on. They returned with no silk goods, but each man had a warm glow inside as he thought of the thirty thousand people who were fed for one week with their combined gift.

There is something in man's nature that causes him to respond to the needs of others. Of course, this higher nature can be dulled, and it often is, but God seems to have placed a capacity for compassion in most people.

As a matter of fact, man appears to be so constituted that his nature demands he give himself in service to others.

In the year A.D. 109 an aqueduct was built by the Roman legions in the city of Segovia, Spain. It was a magnificent piece of engineering. It continued in use for eighteen hundred years, serving the people of that city. Some years ago, however, the Spaniards decided that this ancient structure should be preserved for posterity and be relieved of its centuries of labor. So they laid modern pipelines, and the water ceased to gush through the old aqueduct. Soon it began to fall apart. The hot sun dried the mortar. The aqueduct crumbled and lay in ruins. As long as it served mankind, it was preserved; but when it ceased to be useful, it went to pieces.

I have seen this happen to people. Here is a person who starts out with a fine service motivation for his life. But something happens. He begins to get greedy and self-concerned. Finally, he scorns doing anything for other people that does not "pay off." Whether he knows it or not, his life is lying in ruins just as the Spanish aqueduct did when it no longer served human need.

On the other hand, a self-centered person can find a new and exciting life by beginning to respond to altruistic impulses. Recall Lloyd C. Douglas' novel *Magnificent Obsession*. This is the story of Robert Merrick, a wealthy, selfish, morally bankrupt person who is wasting his life. While he was drunk, he fell from a canoe and almost drowned. He was taken to a nearby hospital where an idealistic nurses' superintendent took an interest in him and helped him to understand that life finds its fulfillment in helping others. He came to see, as someone has said so wisely, that a person who is all wrapped up in himself makes a very small package. So he discovered and began to practice the secret of anonymous service, and his life took on new dimensions.

It is true—selfishness is self-defeating; service is self-expanding. A person who lives only for himself never lives; a person who lives for others finds fulfillment of self. This is written into the very law of our nature.

III

It is the spirit of helpful service that holds together our larger human relationships.

69

In many ways the most remarkable thing about James Michener's *Hawaii* is the account of two families—the Kee family among the Chinese and the Sakagawa family among the Japanese. In each of these there was a close-knit relationship. The parents were willing to undergo any sacrifice to make possible advantages for their children. Family councils were held to determine which child should have an education, and everyone else willingly worked to make that possible. Helping one another was the law of the family.

This is the way God made us. We live at our best in our families when we live not for ourselves, but for each other. The larger human family is like that too. We are far from realizing it, but the problems of the world are not going to be solved until we live for each other.

People can be very trying. One thinks of the cartoon that shows a psychiatrist's office with a dog lying on the couch for therapy. He has a very sad expression on his face. The psychiatrist is a dog also, and as he sits with pencil and pad in hand (or paw!) he is saying to his distraught patient, "May I make a suggestion? Don't judge people, just try to love them." It would be interesting to know what our dogs think of us. We probably are very trying to them! We are very trying to one another!

The breakdown of human relationships in international affairs is not surprising. We don't do very well even in the limited relationships of a family. And we would have to say that the same fault is to be found in both—selfishness. Nations do not serve one another;

they exploit one another to the extent that they can get away with it. When history writes the final word on the Congo and on Cuba, the word "exploitation" will have to be used to account, in part at least, for the turbulence of those lands in this decade. *The Ugly American* revealed an ugly chapter in the world's human relations.

Years ago, when Wendell Willkie journeyed over the earth and wrote his *One World*, he reported that the missionaries had done more to create goodwill for America than the businessmen, for the missionaries were in foreign lands to serve, while the businessmen were there to exploit and to make all they could.

The late Bishop G. Bromley Oxnam used to tell of his experience in Shanghai before the revolution. He visited a Chinese industrialist who was then the president of the YMCA. He was a devout and earnest Christian, and he invited Dr. Oxnam to go through his factory and tell him what he observed that was not Christian. The American churchman did so, reporting on the lack of ventilation in the weaving rooms and the use of child labor and long working hours. The industrialist explained that he was correcting the condition in the weaving rooms, but that nothing could be done about the child labor and the long hours because of the sharp competition of American plants in Shanghai. They too used child labor and required long working hours! He then said to Dr. Oxnam, "When you return to America, tell the businessmen who come to China to practice their Christianity!" The communists

71

found a ready soil for their propaganda when they took over China. American Christian missionaries had said one thing, but American industrialists, after the big profit, practiced another.

In our own time the young nations of the world accept food, loans, and technical assistance from other nations feeling that the "benefactor" is extending the aid not so much from a desire to be helpful as from a desire to gain political or military advantage.

The picture is not all dark, however. A new breakthrough in world human relations was made when the United States established the Peace Corps. These are the "beautiful Americans," not the "ugly Americans." They go to their difficult posts in the same spirit as the Christian missionaries have gone—to serve. They work directly with the people, sharing their misery. Their altruism is genuine, and the sincerity of it comes through. We can be thankful that the Peace Corps is in so many of the struggling nations that are trying to find a new destiny of dignity for every person.

The United Nations was born out of the desire of the human family to help one another. The world health program, the technical assistance program, UNESCO, UNICEF—these and the other agencies of the UN were created not that one nation might have an advantage over another, but that all peoples of the earth might be helped to a fuller life and remain at peace.

Just as the altruistic impulse is essential for every person, the spirit of helpful service is imperative in our social relations if unity and peace are to prevail in the larger human family.

The burden of these words is to say that there is no greater endeavor to which we can give ourselves than that of service. Jesus taught it; he lived it. God wrote the principle of helpful service into our very nature, and it seeks expression in both our personal and our social relationships.

But we who call ourselves Christians have a special reason why service is supreme for us. In a certain town, a man became known for his zeal to help people in need. He had a strange knack of being on hand when anyone was in trouble. When he could help personally, he did so. Also, he knew how to enlist the cooperation and help of others. One day he was asked how he came to be so active in helping other people. He replied, "A man once died for me." Then he told of a perilous situation in which a man tried to save his life, but in doing so lost his own. Thereafter, he said he felt he had to live a double life—one for himself and one for the man who gave his life for him.

I cannot forget that there was One who came into the world "not to be served but to serve, and to give his life" for me.

Prayer
Is Essential

And he told them a parable, to the effect that they ought always to pray.

—Luke 18:1

Jesus prayed at his baptism. He prayed in the wilderness to understand God's will for his life. He prayed for guidance before choosing his disciples. He prayed before revealing his true nature to the world. He prayed before deciding to go to Jerusalem, when to do so meant peril for his life. Prayer was so natural for Jesus that, beyond special occasions and needs, he would break involuntarily into conversation with God. The reality of his spiritual experience so impressed his followers that they beseeched him to teach them how to pray. The prayer life of Jesus was as much a part of him as breathing and the beating of his heart. Without the slightest question, Jesus demonstrated that prayer was essential in his life.

Prayer is a necessary part of our lives too. In Luke's Gospel we read, "And he told them a parable, to the effect that they ought always to pray."

I

We "ought always to pray" for the very basic reason that we have a spiritual nature which must be fed.

We are not animals. Animals follow their instincts and feed and procreate and die. Animals do not set up altars of worship in the forests. They do not set apart special burrows for churches.

For twelve years we had a cocker spaniel we loved very much. She was a good, true friend. A prayer group met in our home on Thursday nights. Rusty, the cocker, attended the prayer meeting. At the end of the evening we always had a closing circle of prayer. We would join hands and stand together in the center of the room. Rusty would slip into the center of the circle and lie there while we had our closing prayer. Rusty was an intelligent dog, but she joined in the prayer meeting not because she wanted to be close to God, but because she wanted to be close to us. Much as we love our animal friends, there is no real evidence to suggest that they have a spiritual nature.

But not so man. "Strange potency, this thing we call

75

Religion! It came into man's world untold centuries ago, and it is still in man's world today. It is still there, deep and tremendous: a mighty draught for a mightier thirst, a vast richness to fill a vaster need. No matter where one turns in time or space, there it is inescapably. Wherever there is a man, there seems to be also a spirit or a god; wherever there is human life, there is also faith." So writes Lewis Browne in *This Believing World*.

Man is incurably religious. Someone has said that he has a God-shaped blank within him.

Man can defile his life. He can get down in the swine pen and eat husks with the pigs, but he knows that the swine pen is not his home. Even in his defilement, he yearns to arise and go to his Father.

Only man is conscious of his sins. Only man yearns for righteousness. The poet may speak of a tree lifting up its leafy arms to pray but that is a poetic expression. Trees do not pray. Animals do not pray. Only man prays—and he does so because there is something in his nature that requires it. There is something in man's nature that hungers and thirsts for fellowship with a Being that is greater than himself.

A very tragic thing happened in Los Angeles a few years ago. A young girl was attending the University of Southern California. She was a disturbed person, who had a compulsion to diet. She would take no nourishment except skimmed milk. She died of malnutrition.

This is what happens to a person who starves his soul. Prayer is the means whereby we feed our deeper nature and quench our spiritual thirst. Prayer is fellowship with God; if we do not have that fellowship, we never become whole persons. Indeed, if we do not commune with God, a very important part of our nature atrophies and dies. For this very basic reason, then, prayer is essential.

II

We "ought always to pray" to redeem the commonplace of our daily living.

I am convinced that many people live a very bored existence. There is no real interest in their lives. They awake every morning at the same time, stumble out of bed, go through the routine of shaving, read the same newspaper, eat the same breakfast, use the same transportation to get to work, go through the identical motions at the desk or counter or workbench, open the lunch box at noon with the same actions, eat the same kind of sandwich, spend the evening watching the same television shows, and go to bed exhausted because the day was so dull! This describes life for millions of people. I am sure that more people die of attrition than of action. Boredom kills more people than overwork.

But it doesn't need to be this way. Grace Noll Crowell writes:

> The common tasks are beautiful if we
> Have eyes to see their shining ministry.

77

The plowman with his share deep in the loam,
The carpenter whose skilled hands build a home,
The gardener working with reluctant sod,
Faithful to his partnership with God—
These are the artisans of life, and oh,
A woman with her eyes and cheeks aglow,
Watching a kettle, tending a scarlet flame,
Guarding a little child—there is no name
For these great ministries, and eyes are dull
That do not see that they are beautiful.

Nicholas Herman—who is known as Brother Lawrence—saw that the common ministries are beautiful. He was a lay brother of the seventeenth century who worked in the kitchen of a monastery in Paris. He regarded himself as a "servant of the servants of God." Thus, he was a very humble man. He learned to "practice the Presence of God" in all his menial tasks, and thus he clothed all that he did with sacramental significance. There wasn't a dull moment in that monastery kitchen. His work was a prayer all day long.

Actually, the experiences of daily living may very well become the instruments for the practice of the Divine Presence. Protestants do not use a rosary as Roman Catholics do. One could, however, make a rosary out of the routine of day-to-day experiences. One could have a prayer for every common event—on waking up, on shaving, on having breakfast, on reading the newspaper, on taking a coffee break, on eating lunch, on closing the desk at the end of the day, on driving one's car, on sitting down to the evening meal, on turning on the television set, on disrobing for bed, on closing one's eyes to go to sleep.

G. K. Chesterton understood this. He wrote:

> You say grace before meals.
> All right
> But I say grace before the play and
>   the opera,
> And grace before the pantomime,
> And grace before sketching, painting, and
>   dancing,
> Fencing, boxing, walking, playing, swimming,
> And grace before I dip the pen in ink.

So! The experiences of every day can become a rosary of spiritual enrichment when prayer is attached to them. Indeed, if we fail to fill the commonplace with prayer, we have not only lost the opportunity to transform the dullness of living, but we have ignored the basic requirement of a spiritual being, which is to walk in fellowship with his Creator.

III

We "ought always to pray" that we might manage the crisis experiences of our lives.

We don't need to be urged to pray when we're in trouble. We do that automatically. Who of us has not sent out a spiritual SOS in a moment of danger or dis-

79

tress? But I'm not thinking of the panicky prayer for God to bail us out of some trouble we've gotten into. Rather, I am thinking of the kind of crisis praying that becomes a Christian—the kind of praying that Jesus himself did when his soul was shaken by the storms of perilous circumstance.

In Gethsemane Jesus prayed a very human prayer. Seeing the shadow of death before him, he prayed: "My Father, if it be possible, let this cup pass from me" (Matt. 26:39). But he went on to say, "Nevertheless, not as I will, but as thou wilt."

On the cross, Jesus prayed another very human prayer. In his agony he cried out, "My God, my God, why hast thou forsaken me?" (Matt. 27:46). But just before he died, he said, "Father, into thy hands I commit my spirit!" (Luke 23:46).

How shall we pray as becomes a Christian in a moment of deep peril? We should pray for courage. Someone has said, "Courage is fear that has said its prayers." Often our greatest enemy in an emergency is panic. When panic sweeps over us, reason is driven out. Many have gone down to defeat in a crisis simply because they lost their heads. Panic can be cast out by prayer.

Thus it was with Billy Hicks of the British Navy. He was assigned to service on the foretop. Previous to his assignment, however, two other men had fallen from the same station and had been killed. There was a superstition of the sea that where two men had lost their lives there would inevitably be a third. Billy

Hicks was well aware of this superstition. He was very much afraid. The night before he was to take his place on the foretop, he was seen working at the telegraph key. The next day he assumed his duty. At the end of the day he came down from the foretop a changed man. His face was radiant, and he stepped from the rigging with remarkable confidence. No one understood why Billy Hicks was such a changed person until another ship reported a strange radio message which had been intercepted the night before. This is what the message said: "God, this is Billy Hicks. I ain't afraid of no bloomin' man or devil. I ain't afraid of no Davy Jones, neither. I ain't like a bawlin' baby a-fussin' at its Dad for sweeties. I don't ask for no favors but jest one. When I strike the foretop tomorrow, let me do it with the nerve of a man what is clean." Prayer had saved Billy Hicks' life by taking away his fear of death. In peril of any kind, we do well to pray for courage.

We should pray also to lay hold upon the wisdom of God. It is the faith of the Christian that God has an answer for every prayer. It may not be the answer we would like. God's wisdom is always higher than ours. But, if we can succeed in purifying the channel of communication between us and God—if we can get self out of the way—eternal wisdom can come through to us.

The problem, of course, is always that of making our personal desires secondary to God's. A very perceptive woman said once, "I think we have the scripture mixed. When we say, 'Speak, Lord, thy servant heareth,' what

81

we really mean is 'Listen, Lord, thy servant speaketh!' "
In time of need we require something more than our
puny wisdom. We must lay hold upon the wisdom of
God.

Further, we should pray that we might tap the
infinite resources of God. Harry Emerson Fosdick
found this when he was a young preacher. He suffered
a severe nervous breakdown. This was followed by a
period of bitter depression. "For the first time in my
life," he wrote in his autobiography, "I faced, at my
wit's end, a situation too much for me to handle. I
went down into the depths where self-confidence becomes ludicrous. . . . In that experience I learned some
things about religion that theological seminaries do not
teach. I learned to pray, not because I had adequately
argued out prayer's rationality, but because I desper-
ately needed help from a Power greater than my own.
I learned that God, much more than a theological
proposition, is an immediately available Resource." This
is what everyone needs to learn in the crisis experiences
of life. God is an immediately available resource.

A young serviceman sat in my study one time. He had
just completed his basic training. I asked him about
some of his experiences in the army. We talked thoughtfully for a long time. Then I asked my young friend
what more he thought the church should be doing for
its young people. The answer he gave was not quite
what I had expected. He said, "I think the church
ought to be teaching young people how to pray." His
army experience had placed him in some very difficult

situations. He had found that deeper spiritual resources were not there when he needed them. In the tug of war for moral mastery he found he needed an invincible anchor man on the side of goodness, and he didn't know how to get that help.

Prayer, as Alexis Carrell has said, releases the most powerful form of energy anyone can know. When a crisis of any kind comes, we must tap this inexhaustible source of power.

How can prayer help us to manage the crisis situations of our lives? It is the means whereby we can secure courage, wisdom, and power.

IV

We "ought always to pray" for a better life for all people.

It is easy to pray for ourselves and for those who are near and dear to us; but, if I understand the spirit of Jesus rightly, we must go beyond that. Piety without social concern is incomplete.

Walter Rauschenbusch was a man of prayer as well as a man of reforming zeal. The two facets of his life were inextricably intertwined. It was no accident that Rauschenbusch wrote both the revolutionary book *Christianizing the Social Order* and another little book of spiritually perceptive *Prayers of the Social Awakening*. From his youth this social prophet was associated with a prayer fellowship called the Brotherhood of the Kingdom. He described some of his prayer experiences as a "real mystical withdrawal into communion with God." His friends disclosed there were times when he was preparing his social prayers that he was "moved to such deep feeling that the tears welled out of his eyes and blotted the paper on which he was writing."

In times past, man had the foolish notion that he could build God's kingdom of righteousness for him. The depravity and brutality of this century has brought us to our knees and to our senses. Now we see that the sickness of society, like a wound in the human body, must heal from within. We must work to improve our world, but if this effort is not accompanied by spiritual disciplines, it will have the effect of giving surface treatment to a deep cancer. We must pray without ceasing, but if our prayers do not include the whole world, they are selfish and vain.

Early in my ministry I was fortunate to have James C. Baker as my Bishop. He has been retired for several years. I remember many things about him—his great interest in the young preachers, his passion for reading and books, and his wise administration. But the one thing I will never forget about Bishop Baker was his prayers. They were deep, searching, and powerful. Almost always the good bishop would end his prayer by lifting up the needs of people everywhere throughout the "whole wide world." As I recall these words, I can hear the very intonation of his voice in my mind.

Thus, we must pray always. We must pray for others as well as for ourselves. We must remember the needs of our brothers and sisters of every race and clime. We must pray for a better life for all people.

Prayer is essential. Our nature requires it. We need it to manage depressing dullness and crushing crises. It is necessary if ever there is to be a better life for all people.

"And he told them a parable, to the effect that they ought always to pray."

Faith
Is Fundamental

*"Why could we not cast it out?" He said to
them, "Because of your little faith."*
—Matt. 17:19-20

Almost immediately after Jesus' great, glowing
experience on the mountain which we call the Trans-
figuration, an event occurred that has some amazing
implications. The disciples had tried to heal an epilep-
tic boy. They were unsuccessful. The boy's father appealed to Jesus, and Jesus healed him. Later, the
disciples asked Jesus why they couldn't heal the boy.
He replied, "Because of your little faith." And then
he said, "If you have faith as a grain of mustard seed,
you will say to this mountain, 'Move hence to yonder
place,' and it will move; and nothing will be impossible
to you."

When Jesus talked about moving a mountain, he was

using an expression that the Jews understood very well. We have difficulty with it today because we are so literal minded. According to William Barclay, a teacher of Jesus' time who expounded and interpreted scripture was often thought of as an "uprooter" or even a "pulverizer" of mountains. Dr. Barclay says that "To tear up, to uproot, to pulverize mountains were all regular phrases for removing difficulties. . . . 'If you have faith enough, all difficulties can be solved, and even the hardest task can be accomplished.'"

Jesus obviously believed that faith is fundamental. Touch the Gospels anywhere, and you find Jesus talking about it or demonstrating it.

Faith, for Jesus, was trust in God. By faith, people were healed of their sicknesses. By faith, people received their sight. By faith, people were restored to their sanity. By faith, people found redemption and release from their sins. Trusting in God, Jesus said, is the cure for anxiety, the answer to our fears. Faith is a way of life. With it we live serenely; without it life is a nightmare of storms and crises that threaten to swamp our little boats.

Let us consider this important quality of life in relation to some of our human problems.

I

Faith and worry.

Worry takes its toll of all of us, some more and some less. We worry about things that have happened, and we worry about things we are afraid are going to happen. There is nothing we can do about the past except to learn a lesson from it. No amount of worrying about it is ever going to change it. You can't go back. The past is not like a roll of film; you can't run it through a film editor and clip out the portion you didn't want to happen. Life isn't made that way. As far as the future is concerned, of course, we must plan as wisely as we know how, but when we have done our best we must then face the future with confidence that things are going to work out all right.

We worry about our loved ones. We should, of course, be concerned about those who are dear to us. We should help them, guide them, and protect them all we can. But when we have done all we can do, we must trust them and allow them the freedom to learn from life as we have. We must trust them to God.

Many of us worry about our health. Of course, we should be concerned enough to follow good health rules, but there is a real sense in which a person can worry himself sick—at least, sicker than he is.

A certain woman made a statistical study of her worries. She tabulated them in a "worry table." This is what she discovered. Forty percent of her worries never happened. She spent that much time spinning her wheels about the future. Thirty percent were about old decisions she could not alter. Twelve percent were about others' criticisms of her, mostly untrue, and made by people who feel inferior. Ten percent were about her health, which worsened because she worried about it. Eight percent of her worries were legitimate, since life does have some real problems to meet. This is probably a pretty good picture of all of us.

Harry Milton Taylor had a nightmarish experience that gives us a clue to victory over worry. He was attending an important conference. The privilege was given to him to introduce two very distinguished ladies, whom he knew well. The moment came, and he rose to his feet and came to the front of the auditorium. The ladies came forward and took their places, one on either side of him. As Taylor introduced the first lady, he bowed to her in courtly manner. Then he stared at her in horror. He suddenly realized that he had called her by the name of the other lady. Not only did he realize it, but everyone in the audience realized it too. He said, "For an endless moment of shock I stood transfixed like a school boy stuck in the middle of a poem. The first lady's name was gone as though I had never known it. My humiliation was complete. That night, as I lay down to sleep, my chagrin leered at me with red eyes. Writhing from side to side, burying my head in the pillow, I could not escape it." Then he said, "I prayed. I said, 'God, you know how I feel, you know how silly I've been, how stupid I am. I did my best and it wasn't good enough. Now the episode is yours. Do with it what you will. May good come of it. Please turn my humiliation into humility.' And," he said, "I went to sleep."

The clue to overcoming worry and anxiety lies in

what this man did. He turned it over to God. And this is faith—the kind of faith Jesus talked about and demonstrated. Faith is trust in God. When a matter worries you, and you have done all you can logically and reasonably do about it, you put it in God's hands. And when you put it in his hands, you don't worry about it anymore. If you find yourself worrying about it again, it simply means that you have taken it back out of God's hands. It means that you don't really trust him, that you don't really have faith in him.

One of the most beautiful passages in the Bible is that found in the sixth chapter of Matthew.

Therefore I tell you, do not be anxious about your life, what you shall eat or what you shall drink, nor about your body, what you shall put on. Is not life more than food, and the body more than clothing? Look at the birds of the air: they neither sow nor reap nor gather into barns and yet your heavenly Father feeds them. Are you not of more value than they? And which of you by being anxious can add one cubit to his span of life? And why are you anxious about clothing? Consider the lilies of the field, how they grow; they neither toil nor spin; yet I tell you, even Solomon in all his glory was not arrayed like one of these. But if God so clothes the grass of the field, which today is alive and tomorrow is thrown into the oven, will he not much more clothe you, O men of little faith? Therefore do not be anxious, saying, "What shall we eat?" or "What shall we drink?" or "What shall we wear?" For the Gentiles seek all these things; and your heavenly Father knows that you need them all. But seek first his kingdom and his righteousness, and all these things shall be yours as well. (Matt. 6:25-33.)

What Jesus is saying here is not that we should be improvident, but that we can learn from the birds of the air and the lilies of the field. And what we learn is this: God takes care of our needs. This doesn't mean that God will take care of all our "wants." There is much that we want that we don't really need. What this means is that we can trust God. We can trust him in everything. The God who made us is not unconcerned about our fate. He will never desert us. And if we are faithful (full of faith) and perceptive, we shall see that he has provided for us in this life and in the life to come.

II

Faith and health.

The Gospels abound in what we call healing miracles. This is not surprising. For at least a quarter of a century the stories and sayings of Jesus were passed on by word of mouth before the Gospel according to Mark was written, and this was the first one to be put into writing. The healing miracles were dramatic. They captured and held the attention of people. It is no wonder that so many of them found their way into the written records which came into being from thirty to sixty years after the crucifixion.

When you study the healing miracles, you find in

almost every case a common ingredient. Let us look at two or three of them.

There was the woman who had been bleeding for twelve years. She was in the crowd where Jesus was. She thought to herself, "If I only touch his garment, I shall be made well." She moved up close to him and touched him. Jesus was aware that something had happened. He asked who it was that had touched him. The woman fell down before him, confessed that she was the one, and told him what had happened. He looked down upon her and said, "Daughter, your faith has made you well" (Luke 8:48).

Luke tells the story of ten lepers. Jesus was on his way to Jerusalem. He was going into a village when he met the lepers. They cried out to him, "Jesus, Master, have mercy on us!" (Luke 17:13). Jesus looked upon them with compassion and said, "Go and show yourselves to the priests." As they went, they were healed. One of them, a Samaritan, came back to thank Jesus. It is an interestnig fact that the other nine did not. The Samaritan praised God, fell at the feet of Jesus, and thanked him. And Jesus said to him, "Rise and go your way; your faith has made you well."

Bartimaeus, the blind beggar, was near the gate when Jesus was leaving the town of Jericho. He heard the commotion of the people and asked what was going on. When he learned Jesus was there, he cried out, "Jesus, Son of David, have mercy on me!" (Mark 10:47). The people tried to shut him up, but he persisted. Jesus called for him and said to the blind beggar,

"What do you want me to do for you?" "Master, let me receive my sight," Bartimaeus pleaded. Jesus looked at him deeply and said, "Go your way; your faith has made you well."

Now what is the common ingredient in all these experiences? *It is the element of faith.* Dr. Charles Laymon, in his book *The Life and Teachings of Jesus,* says, "A study of the procedures which Jesus followed in his healing ministry suggests that the curative power was not in the method itself. Instead, it was in the attitude which the infirm took toward Jesus. The word which describes this attitude best is *faith.*"

Miracles are events whose processes we simply do not understand. When we understand them, they are no longer miracles. But this we understand well: Jesus healed people again and again because of their attitude of faith in him and in his godly power.

Faith is our friend in the operating room of a hospital. When we trust our doctor and submit ourselves to go under his scalpel with confidence, our chances of recovery are vastly increased. On the other hand, when we enter surgery with icy fear gripping our hearts, our bodies are less able to respond to the doctor's care.

Faith is our friend in the convalescent bed. One who believes he is going to get well has a better chance of getting well than another who does not. One who has faith in his doctor and in the medication he gives him— and more important, who has faith in God and trusts him to bring him to complete recovery—will get well sooner than another who does not.

93

Faith is fundamental to health and healing. I do not mean to infer that we can dispense with doctors and medicine and rely solely on faith. I believe God has many ways of healing us when we trust him. I believe the surgeon's knife is a blessed instrument and that the skillful doctor's hands are God's hands to help me when I need them. I believe that the scientific search for the cure for cancer and other dreaded diseases is within the benevolent will and purpose of God. I believe that prayer is an indispensable part of health and healing. I have heard more than one devout physician say in all humility, "I did all I could. I did my best. But I would have to say he is alive today because of a miracle."

I know a woman who has gone through multiple operations. She has spent more time in hospitals than out of them in the past five years. There are times when she gets depressed, of course, because she is human. But she has a lively faith. She trusts God completely. Her bed is her church pew. Her radio is her church. She is cheerful and, in spite of her pain, she is serene. Her faith has not only kept her going; it has kept her growing.

Whether we are sick or not, faith is fundamental to our well-being.

III

Faith and the life that gives meaning to our existence. Jesus was invited into the home of Simon, the Phar-

94

isee (Luke 7:36-50). While he was there a woman, a recognized sinner, came in. She knelt down at Jesus' feet and began to weep. Her tears fell upon his feet. She wiped them with her long hair. Then she took the alabaster flask of ointment she had brought with her and poured its contents on the Master's feet and gently massaged them with her hands. Simon, the Pharisee, was upset about all this. It was not proper. He thought Jesus should have known who this woman was and that it was wrong for him to let her touch him.

While these thoughts were going through his mind, Jesus said to him, "Simon, I have something to say to you."

"What is it, Teacher?" Simon asked.

Then Jesus told Simon about two men who owed another man some money. One of them owed a small amount. The other owed ten times as much. Jesus said that the lender forgave the debts of both these men. Then he asked Simon which of the two men would be the most grateful. Simon said he supposed the one who was forgiven the most. Jesus said he was right. Then he pointed to the woman who had anointed his feet. "Do you see this woman? I entered your house, you gave me no water for my feet, but she has wet my feet with her tears and wiped them with her hair. You gave me no kiss, but from the time I came in she has not ceased to kiss my feet. You did not anoint my head with oil, but she has anointed my feet with ointment. Therefore I tell you, her sins, which are many, are forgiven, for she loved much." Then this wonderful

95

man said to the woman, "Your sins are forgiven. . . . Your faith has saved you, go in peace."

It is hard for us to understand how our faith saves us. We are so accustomed to thinking that we must earn what we get—that we have to earn God's love and favor. But that isn't the case. The life that gives meaning to our existence comes to us as a gift of God's grace.

I knew a woman who was driven out of her mind by a guilt she carried from her childhood. She had pled with God to forgive her. She joined the church and worked in it with all her strength. Everything she did for the church was, in her mind, an act of penance for her sins. She did everything she could to try to be worthy of God's love and the life of serenity and peace she yearned so to possess. But it did not come. She could never feel that God had really forgiven her. I assured her that God would forgive her, but she couldn't believe it.

Faith is fundamental to forgiveness. Unless you can believe in the goodness and grace of God to the point at which you are able to accept the fact that "he is faithful and just, and will forgive our sins and cleanse us from all unrighteousness" (I John 1:9), you cannot know the life of serenity and peace—you cannot know the life that gives meaning to our existence.

This is what the sinful woman in Simon's house did. Jesus observed her penitence. He saw the look of loving trust in her eyes. He said to her, "Your faith has saved you, go in peace."

This is what Paul wrote his letter to the Romans

about. When a person's relationship with God is broken, Paul said, it isn't the law with all its rituals that is going to restore that relationship. Rather, he said, it is an act of faith, a loving acceptance from God's hands of that which no man can ever deserve but which is given freely simply because God loves us with a measureless love. It is true that faith without works is dead, but it is also true that works without faith are futile if we want to find a life that gives meaning to our days. We are saved by faith.

One evening I sat with a man who is a problem drinker. He had blamed all his troubles on his family. He had refused to face the real problem which lay deep within himself. Dejection flowed from every line in his face. He was completely discouraged. He had quit caring. I knew he hated himself, but he didn't dare admit it. He had to keep trying to fool himself that he was all right by the false stimulation of alcohol. He told me there was nothing I could do for him. I replied, "Yes, there is something I can do for you. I can tell you that God loves you—that you are important to him—and that he wants you to have a full life. He sent me to you to tell you this." He lifted his head incredulously. His shoulders squared just a little. A rare hope had been introduced into his unbearable existence. A tiny gleam of encouragement broke through to his tortured soul. The miracle of God's grace was beginning to reach him through an awakening faith.

There is no question about it; faith was a way of life for Jesus. He taught it. He lived it. For him, it

97

meant trusting God. When we trust God as Jesus did, we shall be done with our needless anxieties, we shall be healthier than we are, and we shall know the joy of relationship with God that will transform mere existence into real living.

Possessions
Are Perilous

He went away sorrowful; for he had great possessions.

—Mark 10:22

It is amazing how much Jesus had to say about money and material things. It was one of his most-talked-about subjects. A third of all Jesus' parables and a sixth of all the verses in the Gospels have to do with the right use of possessions.

Jesus wasn't against people having money and material goods. He was deeply troubled about what possessions could do to people, both to the persons who had them and to those who did not.

Jesus was a poor man. He was raised in a humble

home. He worked with his hands at a carpenter's bench. As an itinerant preacher and teacher he had no home, and when a would-be disciple approached him about being a follower, he told him, "Foxes have holes, and birds of the air have nests; but the Son of man has nowhere to lay his head" (Luke 9:58). When he died, he made only one bequest, and that was to place his mother under the care of his dear friend John. His executioners gambled for the only piece of property he had, and that was his robe.

Yes, Jesus was a poor man, but he did not condemn wealth as such. He advised the rich young ruler to sell all he had and give it to the poor in order to test the sincerity of his desire. But when Zacchaeus, another man, offered to make matters right with those he had wronged, Jesus laid no requirement of poverty on him.

He did not set himself up as an economic reformer. There were many things wrong in the society of which Jesus was a part. But he did not choose to lead a movement to liberate the economically depressed, though the application of his gospel leads to that end. He declared that "man shall not live by bread alone" (Matt. 4:4). He was after first things first. So he said, "Seek first his kingdom and his righteousness, and all these things shall be yours as well" (Matt. 6:33).

If I understand Jesus rightly, possessions are perilous because they can so easily separate man from his brother, man from his God, and can so easily possess their possessor.

100

POSSESSIONS ARE PERILOUS

I

Consider the danger of possessions building a wall of separation between people.

There is a street in New York City that is associated with massive wealth. "Wall Street" is a good name for it. It is a narrow street, bordered by tall buildings. The granite and marble structures are occupied by those who seek riches. By the nature of their questing, many of them are men who are walled in from human sympathies.

I recall a man who worked for a large corporation. He held a humble position. He was closer to the laborers in the factory than he was to the management. One day he came into the office of a superior with a suggestion to improve relationships between management and labor. His superior listened to him. Then he said to the man, "Come over here to this window." He did, and they looked out on a parking lot. "Which is your car?" he was asked. He pointed out a modest automobile of considerable vintage. Then his superior said, "Do you see that car?" and pointed to a shiny limousine. "That's what I come to work in. And you presume to tell me what I ought to do!" It is very difficult for some who hold vast possessions to resist building walls of separation between themselves and those who labor for them.

In family life I have seen walls of separation develop between brothers and sisters over an estate after the death of a parent. One of the saddest funerals I ever

101

conducted was one in which the brothers and sisters refused to sit together in the family room because of controversy over the division of the family possessions. They wouldn't even look at each other. When it came time to view the remains in the casket, one part of the family refused to do so with the others.

Jesus knew that possessions could separate men from one another. That's why he told the parable of the rich man and Lazarus.

There was a rich man, who was clothed in purple and fine linen and who feasted sumptuously every day. And at his gate lay a poor man named Lazarus, full of sores, who desired to be fed with what fell from the rich man's table; moreover the dogs came and licked his sores. The poor man died and was carried by the angels to Abraham's bosom. The rich man also died and was buried; and in Hades, being in torment, he lifted up his eyes, and saw Abraham far off and Lazarus in his bosom. And he called out, "Father Abraham, have mercy upon me, and send Lazarus to dip the end of his finger in water and cool my tongue; for I am in anguish in this flame." But Abraham said, "Son, remember that you in your lifetime received your good things, and Lazarus in like manner evil things; but now he is comforted here, and you are in anguish. And besides all this, between us and you a great chasm has been fixed, in order that those who would pass from here to you may not be able, and none may cross from there to us." And he said, "Then I beg you, father, to send him to my father's house, for I have five brothers, so that he may warn them, lest they also come into this place of torment." But Abraham said, "They have Moses and the prophets;

102

let them hear them." And he said, "No, father Abraham; but if some one goes to them from the dead, they will repent." He said to him, "If they do not hear Moses and the prophets, neither will they be convinced if some one should rise from the dead." (Luke 16:19-31.)

What does this mean? It means that the rich man can be so walled in by his wealth that a man in need at his gate evokes no sympathy, and this is a travesty of human relations. Luxury can build a wall so high that a man cannot see the need of his brother.

II

Possessions are perilous not only because they so easily separate man from his brother but because they are so likely to separate man from his God.

How does this come about? William Barclay gives us an insight into this in his commentary on the peril of riches. He says one of the effects of material goods is to encourage in a person a sense of false independence. "If a man is wealthy he is apt to think that everything has its price, that if he wants a thing enough he can buy it, that if any difficult situation descends upon him, he can buy his way out of it. He can come to think he can buy his way into happiness and buy his way out of sorrow. So he comes to think that he can well do without God, that he is quite able to handle life by himself."

This was the point of another story Jesus told about

103

a rich man. We call it the parable of the rich fool. (Luke 12:13-21.) Here was a man who had done so well that he had to tear down his old barns and build larger ones to contain his crops and his many goods. Now, this in itself was not a bad thing. The man was a hard worker, a good planner, and his efforts paid off in increased crops and greater prosperity. The thing that was wrong was that he let this go to his head. He began to think that he had really made it! He was fooled by the illusion that material goods mean security. He said to himself, "Soul, you have ample goods laid up for many years; take your ease, eat, drink, and be merry." It is interesting that Jesus used the word "soul" in this story. He didn't have the prosperous farmer say, "Man, you have ample goods." Instead, he had the farmer say, "Soul, you have ample goods." I think Jesus wanted to make it plain that this man had transferred his security from God to his goods. And that's where he made his mistake! In the moment of his false reliance, God said to him, "Fool! This night your soul is required of you; and the things you have prepared, whose will they be? So is he who lays up treasure for himself, and is not rich toward God."

Not all rich men are rich fools. I have known some (not very many, I must confess) who have never allowed their possessions to blind them to the reality of their ultimate dependence. I had an unusual relationship with a man of great wealth once. He had made his money in oil and real estate. I came to know him in his advanced years, and a deep friendship developed between us. From time to time we would have lunch together just for the pleasure of it. Once a year, in the fall, he would ask me to spend some time with him to talk over his philanthropies (a most unusual experience for a preacher!). He had a fine sense of stewardship. He felt he had been fortunate in the accumulation of material goods and had an obligation to share them thoughtfully. He said once, "I enjoy my giving. I like to plan it. I don't like anyone to tell me what to give to. This is a pleasure I reserve for myself." I felt honored that he wanted to consult me as he planned his gifts. He gave most of his wealth away before he died. He never allowed his possessions to take the place of his God.

Man's security is not in his earthly treasures "where moth and rust consume and where thieves break in and steal" (Matt. 6:19). Man's security is in God. We are on dangerous ground if ever we begin to think otherwise.

III

The ultimate peril of possessions is that they can so easily possess their possessors.

This was the problem of the rich ruler. Here was a fine young man. Mark tells us that Jesus looked upon him in love. He had been well trained in the Jewish law. He was surrounded by material comforts, but he was not satisfied with his life. I do not think Jesus would have required him to sell all that he owned and give it to the poor if he had been willing to. As noted before, he didn't require this of Zacchaeus. But this was a test of discipleship the young man could not pass. He looked at Jesus' invitation, and he looked at his possessions. He weighed the two things in his mind. After doing this, we read, "He went away sorrowful for he had great possessions." In other words, he had become possessed by his possessions.

This brings to mind a story the late Roy Burkhart used to tell. He said a successful businessman came to see his minister. He was obviously upset. He said, "I am considering suicide." The minister asked him why. "I am unhappy," replied the businessman. "Why are you unhappy? You have told me that you make $75,000 a year. I know that you have a wonderful house and that you have a large annuity paid in full. You have two cars. You have everything money can buy." "It makes no difference," said the businessman. "I am unhappy." "Then why don't you give your money away?" asked the minister. "I don't want to be happy quite that badly!" was the answer. The conversation soon came to an end, but the man kept thinking about it. He finally decided to break the enslavement to his material comforts and put God first in his life. He became concerned about the needs of his fellowman and forgot all about suicide. In fact, life became for him an exciting adventure. Unlike the rich young ruler, he refused to be possessed by his possessions.

Now let me say, you don't have to be rich to be possessed by material comforts. I know a lot of middle-class people who have been infected by this disease. We live in a materialistic culture. We don't need to have a lot of money to be caught up in the compulsion to "get ahead." Getting ahead usually means more income, a better car, then two cars, a house in the suburbs, then a boat and a swimming pool and a membership in an exclusive country club. It gets to be quite a rat race after a while. And before you know it, you wake up to find that things are not serving you—you are serving things.

Bennett Cerf is one of my favorite characters. He tells about a housewife who was insatiable in her thirst for keeping up with their friends in the squirrel cage of getting ahead. She complained about the apartment they were living in. She said, "All our friends live ten times better than we do. We simply must move into a more expensive neighborhood." Her husband came home one night shortly after that and said, "Well, we won't have to move after all. The landlord just doubled our rent!"

A man whose income puts him in the upper middle class said to his wife, "Sometimes I wish we didn't have as much as we have. The more we get, the more demands there are. We keep surrounding ourselves with comforts, but are we any happier? We have more money than we've ever had in all our lives, but do we have any more satisfaction out of living?"

That can happen on any income level. A pensioner can be possessed by his possessions, what little there are. A laborer's family can put such a store on creature comforts that their pursuit becomes the controlling passion of their lives. A middle-class family can become enslaved by the status symbols of a "successful American family." And the rich man who owns many bank accounts can be owned by them.

But it doesn't have to be that way. "The love of property," said Boswell, "is strongly implanted in mankind. Property, to be sure, gives us a power of enjoying many pleasures which it can purchase. . . . Let me, however, beware of allowing this passion to take a deep root. It may engross my affections." Wise man!

The secret of managing one's possessions is this: Never allow them to become more important than persons nor to replace God as the object of your ultimate affection. Above all, never allow your possessions to possess you.

God's
Will Is Central

But he said to them, "I must preach the good news of the kingdom of God to the other cities also; for I was sent for this purpose."
— Luke 4:43

Like other people, ministers enjoy talking about their trade. Two young preachers were discussing homiletics one day when suddenly one of them was struck with a thought that had never occurred to him before. He said, "I wonder what Jesus preached about most?"

The preaching of Jesus was centered in many subjects. He talked often about God, the Father. He spoke of nature, money, hypocrisy, faith, prayer, forgiveness, and love. But none of these subjects, great as they are, constituted the central theme of Jesus' thought. What Jesus preached about most was the kingdom of God.

Look at the record. The purpose of the Master's ministry was firmly set in the early days of his public life. Upon his return from the wilderness experience, Jesus learned that John the Baptist had been imprisoned. "From that time," reports Matthew, "Jesus began to preach, saying, 'Repent, for the kingdom of heaven is at hand'" (Matt. 4:17). Mark puts it somewhat differently, but the common element of the two reports is unmistakable. "Now after John was arrested, Jesus came into Galilee, preaching the gospel of God [the King James Version says, "the gospel of the kingdom of God"], and saying, 'The time is fulfilled, and the kingdom of God is at hand; repent, and believe in the gospel.'" (Mark 1:14-15.)

Luke tells of Jesus' going to Capernaum, where he was exceedingly popular, shortly after this. The people wanted him to stay there. They followed him to his place of retreat to beseech him. And this is what he said to them: "I must preach the good news of the kingdom of God to the other cities also; for I was sent for this purpose." At the end of Jesus' second preaching tour in Galilee, Luke describes his work by saying, "He went on through cities and villages, preaching and bringing the good news of the kingdom of God" (Luke 8:1).

Of the forty-four parables Jesus told, sixteen refer directly to the kingdom of God. Eighty-nine times in the record preserved by the four Gospels, the words "kingdom of God" or "kingdom of heaven" were on the lips of Jesus. Undoubtedly, this is what Jesus preached about most!

I

One does not pursue this matter very far, however, until he comes squarely up against the question, "What is the kingdom of God?"

In all honesty, we must admit this is not an easy question to answer. "Jesus never defined what he meant by 'the kingdom of God' or 'the kingdom of heaven,'" says Milo Connick, a New Testament teacher. "Consequently its nature and nearness have become matters of heated dispute."

To answer the question, "What is the kingdom of God?" puts us in the well-known predicament of the blind men and the elephant. One man, you will recall, feeling his way toward the beast, happened to touch the elephant's trunk. He said, "Lo, an elephant is very like a snake." The second blind man encountered the animal's tail and said, "Lo, an elephant is like a rope." The third man touched the mastodon's massive leg and said, "Lo, an elephant is very like a tree." And the fourth unseeing man felt the animal's side and declared, "The elephant is very like a wall." They were all correct according to their individual experience with the elephant, but their conclusions were fragmentary, not comprehensive.

Thus, one person walks up to the sayings of Jesus

111

and lays his hand on the remark, "It is the Father's good pleasure to give you the kingdom" (Luke 12:32), and he says, "Lo, the kingdom of God is the Father's gift; it does not come by man's effort." But another person confronts the statement of Jesus, "Not everyone who says to me, 'Lord, Lord,' shall enter the kingdom of heaven, but he who does the will of my Father" (Matt. 7:21), and he says, "Lo, the kingdom of God is man's achievement." A third person walks up to the sayings of Jesus and lays his hand on the Master's remark that "the kingdom of God is within you" (Luke 17:21), and he says "Lo, the kingdom of God is individual. It is an inner experience." But still another person encounters the words of Jesus that "the kingdom of heaven is like leaven which a woman took and hid in three measures of meal, till it was all leavened" (Matt. 13:33), and he says, "Lo, the kingdom of God is social. It permeates all of life. It is a social hope." Here is another individual who runs across the saying of Jesus that "the kingdom of God is at hand" (Mark 1:15), and he declares, "Lo, the kingdom of God is already present. It is here." But another person will find the counsel Jesus gave his followers to look forward to the day when they will hear him say, "Come, O blessed of my Father, inherit the kingdom prepared for you" (Matt. 25:34), and he will insist that the kingdom of God is yet to come. It is a future event.

So! While the idea of the kingdom of God is so significant that it was the Master's magnificent devotion, to most of us it is only an idea cloaked in immense confusion, an idea so big that we, like the blind men and the elephant, can only comprehend parts of it. What is the kingdom of God? Jesus said it is this, it is that, it is something else. It doesn't seem to make sense, but it does.

II

There is a key that transforms the mystery of the kingdom of God into comprehension.

This key is found in the prayer Jesus used to instruct his disciples. He said,

Pray then like this:

> Our Father who art in heaven,
> Hallowed be thy name.
> Thy kingdom come,
> Thy will be done,
> On earth as it is in heaven (Matt. 6:9-10).

Reflect on these important phrases but expecially on two of them. "Thy kingdom come, thy will be done." These are not two phrases saying different things. They are one and the same. The second merely explains and elaborates the first. They are synonymous! Georgia Harkness says, "These words must explain the meaning of the kingdom, just as the phrase 'the communion of saints' explains the term 'the holy catholic church.'"

Here then is the key we are searching for, the key that unravels the mystery of the kingdom of God.

113

Whenever and wherever the will of God is done, there is the kingdom of God.

Thus, we see that the kingdom of God is personal, for whenever and wherever the will of God is done in individual life, the kingdom is there. It is also social, for whenever and wherever the will of God is done in social situations, in race relations, in economic affairs, in international matters, the kingdom of God is there. The kingdom of God is here in this present moment, for no moment is entirely absent from the effort on the part of someone to do the will of the Father. It is also coming, for succeeding generations will be about the Father's business also—more faithfully, we hope, than we of this generation have been. The kingdom is God's gift, for he reveals his will to men. But it is also man's achievement, for it takes man's answering response to complete the process. Indeed, whenever and wherever God's will is done, his kingdom has come.

I have seen the kingdom of God many times. I have seen it in my study as I have talked with men and women who were sweating out destiny-laden decisions. Here, for example, is a young man. He is aware of unique powers surging through himself. His mind is as sharp as a razor. He has the potential for pushing back the borders of man's knowledge. He is humble about his brilliance. He knows he could use these special abilities of his for personal gain. But he turns from this as Pierre and Marie Curie turned from commercializing radium and profiting personally from it. And he says, "I believe it is God's will that I use these talents of

114

mine, not for myself but for the good of mankind."
And, as the young man says that, the kingdom of God
is in that room, sitting in that chair!

I have seen the kingdom of God in the eyes of
persons who, because of limitations accepted and util-
ized without resentment, wear the red badge of courage. Every parish minister has seen such people. Without
complaint they keep on saying day after day, "What is
it, Father, you are trying to tell me? Whatever it is, I
will do it." Thus, I have seen the kingdom of God in a
hospital bed, in a humble home where death has struck
down a beloved husband and father, in a marriage
counselor's office where a young couple are seeking to
work out their adjustments to each other for the sake of
their children.

I have seen the kingdom of God in church board
meetings. I have seen its opposite too at times! Here
is a group of responsible officials of the local church.
They are facing a serious matter. They have brought
their best judgment to bear upon it. And now they
say, "Our judgment is frail and full of our own self-
will. Let us be sure that what we do is pleasing to God!"

When Frank Laubach left Columbia University and
with his young wife headed for the Philippines for
missionary service, some of his hometown people re-
marked, "Those islands are full of wild men with
rings in their noses. Why doesn't Frank have sense
enough to stay home and become a good dentist like
his father!" But Frank Laubach went to the Philippines
to work among the Moros. He found he couldn't

do much until he learned the native language which had never been reduced to writing. He developed an alphabet and a simple system of words and phrases that would help him to remember the language. The Moros were fascinated. They too learned to read and write. This was the beginning of Laubach's mission to the illiterates of the world, the unawakened masses comprising three fifths of the human race. It has been said that Laubach's discovery, which has now driven back the wilderness of illiteracy in more than a hundred different countries, is going to rank with and may even surpass nuclear fission among the great events of this century. Who can estimate the growth of the kingdom of God through a man named Laubach whose life is utterly dedicated to the will of God? I have seen the kingdom of God in Frank Laubach's face!

I have seen the kingdom of God in Hong Kong at the Church World Service feeding centers. A Church World Service official took me to several of these centers. I looked into the faces of hundreds of refugees from mainland China who were trying to find a new life in Hong Kong. The children came with their little buckets to receive a ration of milk and a few biscuits. With love and concern, the Church World Service workers distributed the food to the people. I kept thinking of the words of Jesus, "As you did it to one of the least of these my brethren, you did it to me." Knowing it is God's will that we help our brothers in need, I saw the kingdom of God there in Hong Kong!

Indeed, times without number, whether we know

it or not, we have seen the kingdom of God. We have seen it in persons both humble and great. We have seen it in events both obscure and illustrious. Why? Because the kingdom of God is at hand whenever and wherever the Father's will is done.

III

We have asked a question, "What is the kingdom of God?" and we have found a key of understanding. Now let us come to an exceedingly important matter—the challenge to live the kingdom of God life, the challenge to pursue the will of God in all our relationships, personal and corporate.

This is where the rub comes. It is hard to know, and it is even harder to do the will of God when we know it.

There have been times when I have been quite sure that I understood the will of God for my life in some given situation but later found I was wrong. Why is it so difficult? I believe it is difficult because subjective perception of God's will is frequently untrustworthy. God is always trying to come to us, but he must come to us through our clever self-deceptions. He comes to us through layer upon layer of self-interest. This is why it is so difficult for us really to know the will of God.

If this is hard for an individual, think how much harder it is to try to understand God's will in a complex social or international situation. Pick up your newspaper and read about the latest international crisis.

117

Then ask yourself the question, "What is the will of God in that particular situation?" Try to put yourself in the chair of the President of the United States. He is concerned to do what needs to be done for the welfare of our country. He must make decisions that will affect the lives and destinies of many people not only of this country but of other countries of the world. What is God's will for the President of the United States as he makes these decisions? What is God's will for the Congress of the United States? What is God's will for the United Nations? These are not easy questions to answer.

Recall the names of towns and cities which were battlegrounds for the civil rights movement in our time. Little Rock. Montgomery. Meridian, Mississippi. Philadelphia, Mississippi. Selma, Alabama. Not all the people who live in these towns and cities are members of the Ku Klux Klan or the White Citizens Councils. Many are earnest Christians. They have a genuine concern for the Negro people. They don't like what is going on. What is the will of God for them, in their situation? They are in the minority. How can they advance the cause of justice when the climate of opinion is against them in their town? I ask myself, "If I had been a pastor in one of those towns, what would I have done? Would I have understood the will of God? If I had understood it, would I have done it?"

We must have some guidelines if we are to understand what God's will is in given situations. At the risk of

118

oversimplifying, let me suggest three: communion, common sense, and Christ.

By communion I do not mean the sacrament of the Lord's Supper. I mean the effort on the part of an individual to live in the presence of God so earnestly that the Father's will can come to him through a sensitive spirit. I mean prayer and meditation and reflective reading of the Bible and of the writings of the spiritual giants of the ages. But we must recognize the danger of misunderstanding the will of God by direct revelation. And so we must check this.

This brings us to common sense. Dr. Leslie Weatherhead in *The Will of God* tells of a man who said to him, "I prayed for advice, but nothing happened, and I got no answer to my prayers; so I used my common sense." In Marc Connelly's play *Green Pastures*, one of the characters says, "I think de Lawd expects us to figure out a few things for ourselves." I am sure this is so. I am sure God intends us to use our brains, our reason, our intelligence to try to understand his will. Certainly the subjective perception of God's will in any given situation should be checked by common sense.

But common sense needs to be checked too. Common sense will cause us to compromise. It will cause us to save our skins. Our reason is often clouded by subjective feelings too. And so we must come to the third guideline—Christlikeness. In Stanley Jones's little booklet *How Does God Guide Us?* he says, "When in doubt, do the most Christ-like thing and you will not go wrong. If any guidance seems to be at variance at any point with what you see in Christ, then doubt that guidance, for it cannot be of God, however implemented it may be by reason or emotion. God cannot ask you to do an un-Christlike thing—that would be contrary to his own nature."

To know God's will is not easy. To do it after we know it is harder still. But the challenge is ever before us to be spiritually sensitive, intellectually disciplined, and morally controlled by the spirit of Christ.

Jesus came preaching the kingdom of God. He not only preached it, he lived it. Our calling is to preach it and to live it too.

Love
Is Unbeatable

Love your enemies, and do good, and lend, expecting nothing in return; and your reward will be great, and you will be sons of the Most High.

—Luke 6:35

Love has a language that is all its own. The late Dr. Elmer E. Helms used to tell of his reunion with his small son after an extended absence because of illness. It was early in his ministry, and Dr. Helms had spent long months in a sanitarium. Finally, the day arrived when he was to return home. The boy, whose mother had died when he was an infant, had been living with his grandmother. Careful instructions had

121

been given to the lad, who was to go to the train to meet his father. He would recognize him because he would be on crutches. The young father was informed that his son would be wearing a bright red cap. The moment arrived, and one can imagine a touching scene when the boy and his dad greeted each other after the weary months of separation. They climbed into a waiting carriage and soon were delivered at the grand-mother's home. The parlor doors were opened, for this was an important occasion. The convalescent man went into the parlor and eased himself into a large, comfortable chair, and the boy climbed upon his lap. He nestled his head in the curve of his father's neck, and they sat in this fashion for a long time, without a word being spoken. At last, the boy lifted his head and slid down from his father's lap saying, "Gee, Dad, haven't we had a wonderful visit!" In telling this story, Dr. Helms would say, "In what language did we visit?" And you knew the answer before he gave it. "It was the language of love!"

Jesus did not articulate the principle of the invincible nature of love very often. For the most part, he left this truth to be proclaimed by the special language of love—a language without words. Perhaps the expression that comes closest to a definite statement of the idea is found in Luke when Jesus said, "Love your enemies, and do good, and lend, expecting nothing in return, and your reward will be great, and you will be sons of the Most High." Beyond anything he ever said, however, it was through the experience

of the cross and the resurrection that Jesus declared
the truth so profoundly. On Calvary he gambled love
against force and won. Studdert-Kennedy said:

> And sitting down, they watched Him
>   there,
> The soldiers did;
> There, while they played with dice,
> He made His sacrifice,
> And died upon the Cross to rid
> God's world of sin,
>
> He was a gambler, too, my Christ,
> He took His life and threw
> It for a world redeemed.
> And ere His agony was done,
> Before the westering sun went down,
> Crowning that day with crimson crown,
> He knew that He had won.

I

As we begin to examine this idea Jesus demonstrated
so well, we soon come to see that it is not just any kind
of love that is unbeatable.

Certainly we would rule out halfhearted love. Sometimes we deceive ourselves as to the quality of our
affections. We are like the boy who wrote an effusive
love letter to his girl friend and said, "Darling, I love
you. My love is like a red, red rose that blooms for you
alone. It is like the nectar of the gods. It is my soul's

delight. Because of it, I would travel to the ends of the earth for you. I would dare the greatest dangers. I would fight my way to your side though giants should oppose me. Through storm and flood and fire I would persevere to reach you. Accept this as the expression of my undying love. Yours forever, John. P. S. If it doesn't rain tonight, I will be over to see you." Half-hearted love is out.

Selfish love is out also. It is exceedingly difficult to act from pure motives with no taint of self-interest.

John Ruskin, in spite of his great creative talents, lived a very tragic life. In fact, a biography was written of him with the title, *The Exquisite Tragedy: An Intimate Life of John Ruskin*. His parents were very ambitious for him. They loved him but, as sometimes is the case with parents, they loved the dream of what they wanted him to be more than they loved the boy himself. They would not allow him to make decisions for himself, and when he did, often as not, these were revoked by his parents. Ruskin found it hard to love anyone because his experience of love from his parents was such a tangled one. He said once, "When affection did come, it came with violence, utterly rampant and unmanageable, at least by me who never before had anything to manage." I am sure Ruskin's parents meant well, but their love for this son was a confused love.

I have seen parents who have come to the parting of the ways in marriage fight over the custody of their children. They may insist they love their children, but too often their real motive is to "punish" a mate

124

who has hurt them. I have known people who have thrown themselves into humanitarian causes with great zeal without really loving the people they were trying to help. Unconsciously, they were seeking recognition. I have known preachers who entered the ministry and who failed in their work essentially because they didn't really love the people they were seeking to serve. Without recognizing it, they were seeking their own fulfillment. They needed to feel important. They enjoyed the "star" role in which ministers are inevitably cast.

Yes, I am sure it is hard to keep love pure and unstained by self-interest. And I am sure of another thing: That kind of love is weak and vulnerable. That kind of love won't stand up.

II

It is the kind of love Jesus exemplified that is invincible and desirable—total love that is drained of self.

Allan Hunter in a book called *Courage in Both Hands* tells the story of Merlin Bishop, an American missionary in China, who was in charge of a mission school during the second World War. The Japanese invaders came and the village was captured. In fact, the village became the field headquarters for the Japanese army, and Merlin Bishop knew that it would be a matter of time until the officers would be demanding the mission buildings for their use. The military delegation came and ordered the keys to be turned over to them. Bishop declined to obey—politely, but firmly, explaining that these buildings belonged to an American mission board, and he was not at liberty to hand them over to anyone else. After an hour and a half of discussion in which the missionary remained adamant, but friendly and courteous, the military delegation departed. But this was not to be the end of the matter. They came again and again, and it taxed Bishop's patience to go through this experience over and over.

One day when they came, the missionary sensed that this delegation would be more difficult. His courteous and patient arguments only seemed to inflame the soldiers. Finally, the officer in charge said, "Surrender the keys, or we shoot you!"

"I have told you how it is," Bishop replied quietly. "I wish you no harm, but I cannot do what you ask."

The officer lined up three men facing the missionary, and the soldiers raised their rifles to their shoulders. "Surrender the keys!" the officer said grimly.

"I cannot. . . . I have told you I cannot. I have no hatred against you, only the friendliest feelings for you. But I cannot give you the keys." There was veiled admiration and baffled wonder in the eyes of the soldiers.

"Aim!" the officer said. His voice was gruff as he spoke once more to the missionary. "Your last chance," he said. "Surrender the keys!"

Bishop looked without malice into the eyes of each man. Patiently he said, "I cannot. You know that I cannot." The moment was electric. It was as if time stood still. The officer's determination was broken. The soldiers lowered their rifles and finally broke into sheepish embarrassed grins.

But the moment of danger was not over entirely. One soldier, apparently ashamed of his weakness, regripped his rifle and glared at the missionary. Merlin Bishop prayed within himself, "Father—a little more love. Let me show a little more love." The soldier lunged at him with fixed bayonet. "He came fast," Bishop says, "and he came hard. At the last instant when the point of his bayonet was not a foot from me, I dodged. He missed, and the force of his charge carried him up to me. I reached around him, and with my right hand grabbed the butt of his rifle. With my left hand I grasped him against me. I was taller than he, and he had to look up at me. When our eyes met, his face was contorted with fury. Our glances locked and held for seconds that seemed ages long. Then I smiled down at him, and it was like a spring thaw melting the ice on a frozen river. The hatred vanished, and after a sheepish moment, he smiled back!"

It was all over—and shortly afterward the soldiers were having tea with the missionary in his quarters. They were a little bewildered about it all, for they had met a force that was greater than they understood.

We are dealing with something here that is only beginning to be understood. Harry and Bonaro Overstreet in writing about the creative handling of conflicts said, "Of all the powers man has released in the world none has proved more surprising than has ra-

127

tional good will applied to a situation where the stage is set for hostile self-defense and retaliation."

In 1918 Pitirim A. Sorokin was imprisoned and condemned to death by the Russian Communist government. For six weeks he lived under the constant strain of expecting to be shot. He saw his friends executed. Miraculously his life was spared. But he endured other painful experiences and saw unbelievable human bestiality for four years before he was delivered. During those days he came to a conviction that "cruelty, hatred, violence, and injustice never can and never will be able to create a mental, moral, or material millennium. The only way toward it is the royal road of all-giving creative love, not only preached but consistently practiced." Many years after this, Sorokin established the Harvard Research Center in Creative Altruism, feeling that someone needed to "devote himself to a study of the miracle of love." Scholarly and scientific inquiry confirmed the conviction which had impressed itself upon Sorokin when his life was precarious under the Bolsheviks. The research specialists employed by the center rolled up a preponderant weight of historical evidence that love has operated in human relations as a powerful redemptive force that can overcome fear, hate, and violence.

It is this redemptive love that is invincible—love that is total and is void of the impurities of self. It is the kind of love we see exemplified in Jesus.

It was what Nicodemus saw in the light of a crescent moon as Jesus talked to him far into the night. It was

what the disciples saw on Jesus' face as he healed the
sick, gave vision to the blind, and brought a radiant
joy back into the lives of men and women who had
been released from the quicksand of sin. It was what
Zacchaeus saw in the Master as he walked by under the
sycamore tree and later sat with the tax collector in his
house. It was what a woman saw reflected in the tears
that fell upon Jesus' feet before she brushed them away
with her hair. It was what Pilate saw in the Galilean's
eyes, as this strange man stood silently, hauntingly,
before the magistrate. It was what the sickened throng
saw on the dying face of the man on the cross when his
lips moved with a final effort to say, "Father, forgive
them; for they know not what they do" (Luke 23:34).
It was what the Roman captain saw as he watched Jesus
die and felt compelled to say, "Truly this man was a
son of God!" (Mark 15:39).

III

We confront a plain, realistic fact, however, that must
not be ignored. Sometimes love seems to lose.

Perhaps there will come to your mind, even now, an
instance in which a person known to you has had no
malice, nothing but good will, but his love has not
availed to change another who seems bent on bringing
harm. "What about that?" you ask. Well, there are two
things that should be said to this. One is that we can
never know when a person's love toward another is
pure and without taints of selfishness. We cannot even

129

judge that of ourselves. Oftentimes we think we are acting from pure motives when we are not. It is so easy to deceive ourselves. And if we cannot know this about ourselves, how can we expect to know it of others? Needless to say, when one acts from pure and undefiled motives of love and good will, others will respond to him in like manner more times than not. Even so, and this is the second thing that needs to be understood, there will be times when pure love will seem to fail. This was true in the case of Judas. Jesus loved Judas with an undefiled love, but Judas betrayed him. Jesus loved all people—even the haughty scribes and Pharisees, but it was these religious leaders who sought his death. Even the love of Jesus did not always win— immediately. "How about that?" you ask. There is a Danish hymn that gives us an answer:

> That cause can neither be lost nor stayed
> Which takes the course of what God has made,
> And is not trusting in walls and towers,
> But slowly growing from seeds to flowers;

> Each noble service that men have wrought
> Was first conceived as a fruitful thought;
> Each worthy cause with a future glorious,
> By quietly growing becomes victorious.

> There by itself like a tree it shows:
> That high it reaches as deep it grows:
> And when the storms are its branches shaking,
> It deeper root in the soil is taking.

> Be then no more by a storm dismayed,
> For by it the full grown seeds are laid;

And though the tree by its might it shatters,
What then, if thousands of seeds it scatters!

Love that is true to itself and dies in an effort to
redeem others has a strange quality of becoming mag-
nified in its ultimate power. This is what happened to
Jesus. This is the essential meaning of the cross. Love
was crucified that day, but even as they killed it and
stamped it out like a troublesome grass fire, it broke
loose again and finally swept across the world. This is
the manner in which love is finally unbeatable. Following its crucifixion there is always a resurrection with
power!

The trouble with us is that we are too impatient for
results. We can't wait! We want goodness and love to
pay off every Saturday night! We want to see things
happen! We are too impatient to wait a hundred or a
thousand years to see the ultimate triumph of love.
When Jesus expressed his law of love and mercy, he
said, "Love your enemies, and do good, and lend,
expecting nothing in return; [Dr. Goodspeed translates
this last phrase differently; he says, "never despairing"],
and your reward will be great, and you will be sons of
the Most High." Jesus did not say, "Love your enemies,
and do good, and lend, for thus you will turn all your
enemies into friends overnight; this is a clever formula
for human relationships that always works." No, he
didn't say that, because it isn't true. This formula
doesn't always work. If it did we would fall into the

131

temptation of using it without real love just to gain our ends. What Jesus did say was: "[Do this] and your reward will be great, and you will be sons of the Most High." What reward? The reward of inner satisfaction—the satisfaction of knowing that you have been true to yourself—the reward that comes to a man who has acted in a godly manner, who has lived up to the high standard of a "son of the Most High."

Jesus was saying this is the way God deals with those who hate and oppose him. He loves his enemies. He does good to them. He lends them everything he possesses—the fullness of the earth, rain, and sunshine that are no respecters of persons whether they be good or bad. He goes the second mile with everyone. We could never demand the goodness that God so freely bestows upon us. None of us could ever really merit God's favor. But he gives it to us freely, without expecting anything in return, with a divine love that is too great for us to comprehend. And when we deal with our enemies and those who oppose us in the same manner, our conduct and action may not always pay off in immediate returns, but we shall have our rewards—the greatest of which is to know that we are acting like children of the most high God. All anti-love forces carry within them the seeds of their own defeat and destruction. All love forces carry within them the seeds of their ultimate triumph. This is what Jesus proclaimed and articulated with his life.

Herman Melville, who wrote the thrilling sea story *Moby Dick*, wrote another novel about the sea, *Billy*

Budd, which later was made into a play. The theme of the story is that absolute good and absolute evil cannot live in this world together. According to Melville, "Each must destroy the other, for human life is a compromise that follows the middle way."

The setting of the play is a British warship in 1798. Billy Budd is a naïve, appealing young sailor who always sees the best in everyone, even in the cruel and despicable character of Claggart, the master-at-arms. Billy Budd seeks to break through the hardness of Claggart with the sheer power of his goodness and faith in people. Claggart is determined to resist the young sailor's appeal, and in turn to break him and kill him. Thus, during the play, you see this life-and-death struggle between Budd, symbol of absolute goodness, and the master-at-arms, who is the epitome of absolute evil.

In an effort to get him into trouble, Claggart fabricates an evil lie about Billy Budd and tells it to Captain Vere in Budd's presence. Billy is so shocked by this bald lie that he cannot speak. His lips try to form words of denial, but he succeeds only in stuttering. In complete frustration to express himself, and in a moment of passionate righteous indignation, Billy strikes Claggart, who falls to the deck and lies still. Captain Vere calls for the surgeon and sends Budd to the stateroom to wait. The surgeon examines Claggart and reports him dead.

Captain Vere receives the surgeon's report with horror. In a flash, he perceives that Claggart has re-

133

ceived his just deserts, but as captain of the ship he is placed in the unhappy position of having to judge the young sailor. Captain Vere says to himself, "The divine judgment of Ananias! Struck dead by the Angel of God . . . and I must judge the Angel. Can I save him? Have I that choice?"

An officer's court is summoned, and after an agonizing conflict between duty and personal sympathy, Captain Vere finally decrees that Budd must die for striking and killing a superior officer. At the hour of sunrise, Billy Budd, symbol of goodness, is to hang from the main yard.

The final scene is most dramatic. All on the ship have been summoned to hear the sentence and witness the execution. The men of the crew are stunned. They almost break into mutiny to release Billy Budd. The young sailor starts to mount the mainmast. He is smiling and his essential goodness is luminous. He turns, as he mounts the ropes, and with a smile of forgiveness says, "God bless Captain Vere!" Vere and all the crew are profoundly shaken. Then Budd starts climbing up the rigging to the mainmast. His face reflects pure goodness as he climbs into the growing light of the sunrise and to the death which has been decreed.

Thus, Herman Melville made his point—that absolute good and absolute evil must destroy each other. And yet, one knows that Melville was wrong, for in the moment of facing its destruction, goodness forgave and rose into the sunrise in spiritual triumph!

Love Is Unbeatable

The words of Edwin Markham come to mind.

> He drew a circle that shut me out—
> Heretic, rebel, a thing to flout.
> But Love and I had the wit to win;
> We drew a circle that took him in!

This is the sense in which Jesus proclaimed that love is unbeatable.

Life
Is Eternal

Because I live, you will live also.
—John 14:19

The resurrection of Christ nineteen centuries ago was more than the defeat of sin and evil by purity and good. It was the confirmation of man's hope for immortality. Someone said of Christopher Columbus that the instinct of an unknown continent burned in him. That instinct was confirmed by his voyage across the ocean to the new world. Man bears an instinct of a new world in his breast—a world unlimited by time and space. That instinct was confirmed when Jesus rose from the dead. "Yet a little while," Jesus said, "and the world will see me no more, but you will see me; because I live, you will live also."

If the disciples had had ears to hear, they would have understood what Jesus believed about death and eternal life. On more than one occasion the Master expressed it by dramatic action and well-chosen words.

One day, when he felt the mood of crisis closing in upon him, he said to his disciples, "The hour has come for the Son of man to be glorified. Truly, truly, I say to you, unless a grain of wheat falls into the earth and dies, it remains alone; but if it dies, it bears much fruit" (John 12:23-24). By this Jesus was saying that death is like a dormant period of a seed before it breaks forth into its fullest possibilities of life.

On two occasions, when Jesus was brought to homes where death had visited, he amazed his friends by the manner in which he regarded the grim situation. He stood over a young girl who had died and said, "The girl is not dead but sleeping" (Matt. 9:24). At another time, when Jesus had learned of the illness that was to be fatal to Lazarus, he told the disciples they must go to the home of his dear friends, Mary and Martha, for said he, "Our friend Lazarus has fallen asleep, but I go to awake him out of sleep" (John 11:11). By these events and words, Jesus was saying death is like a sleep.

When Jesus was on the cross, one of the thieves cursed him, but the other turned to the Master seeking pardon, and Jesus responded to him by saying, "Today you will be with me in Paradise" (Luke 23:43). By this, Jesus was saying death is like taking a journey.

Thus it was always with Jesus. In his mind death was

not the dreaded specter people usually make of it. His belief in the continuation of life was so profound that death became a relatively minor matter, like a seed lying dormant in the ground, or like going to sleep, or like taking a journey. Death, for him, was an incident, and life was eternal. What if we really believed, as Jesus did, that life is forever? Some are frankly skeptical of it. A man once said to me, "I believe that what a person does in his life lives on in other people, but to think that I have a soul that keeps on living forever— well, I just can't buy that!" But this isn't the problem with most people. Most people I know say they believe in immortality, but I am not sure they really do. They can say it with their lips, but the way they live denies what they say.

What would happen if we could really believe, as Jesus did, that life is eternal?

I

For one thing, we would stop being afraid of death.

I recall some descriptive music on the radio when I was a college student. It made a tremendous impression on me. A commentator described the dramatic action. A woman was lying on her bed in illness. The muted music portrayed the dreamy state of one who floated in and out of consciousness. The music became louder and there was a rhythmic swing to it that suggested a dance. The woman rose from her bed and was swept into the arms of a man who swung her through the dance with breathless motion. The tempo increased to a fever pitch. And then the music subsided until it became as faint as a distant memory. In this moment the woman looked up into the face of her dancing partner. The violins voiced her scream of terror as she recognized the face of death. Is this not the way most people regard death—as a fearful specter whose clutches we must escape as long as we can?

I do not mean to suggest that people should be reckless and court death as though it were more desirable than life. I am sure God intends us to enjoy life on this planet to the full. What we have in this existence is a prelude to eternity, a rehearsal for glory. We should live it to the full as long as we can. What I do mean to say is that when we think of death in the way Jesus did, we will approach that experience, whenever it comes at whatever age, with the same calm assurance with which we open a garden gate knowing there is entrancing beauty beyond it.

On an airplane trip my seatmate was a man who owned a chain of theaters in the West. I discovered in visiting with him that he was a Roman Catholic who didn't work at his religion very faithfully. It was during the winter, and when we arrived over Dallas, we found an extremely low ceiling. It was necessary for the plane to circle in the fog for some time until the weather cleared for landing. We had been told before taking off that there was some question about landing at Dallas because of icy runways, so we were aware of that danger too as we circled in the clouds. My seatmate was nervous and fidgeted endlessly beside me. Being tired and without fear, I reclined in my seat and took a short nap. When I awoke, we were still circling, and my friend was in quite a mental state. With beads of nervous sweat standing out on his face, he said in a tone of utter exasperation, "How can you do it? How can you be relaxed and sleep with us flying around in this awful soup and no telling what will happen when we try to land!" I talked with him about my faith in God and how our lives, whether here or hereafter, are in the hands of God. I told him I always say a prayer for the captain and his crew and for all the people on the plane when I take my seat. I commend them all, including myself, into God's loving hands. I don't worry about it. He looked at me incredulously. But I noticed when finally we made an excellent landing and were rolling to a stop on the runway, my friend glanced at me with a sheepish grin and then crossed himself fervently.

What unnecessary agonies we mortals cause ourselves because of the fear of death! How we need to remember the serenity of Jesus when he said, "Let not your hearts be troubled; believe in God. . . . Because I live, you shall live also."

When you believe as Jesus did that life is eternal, that immortality is not a mirage that mocks us on the merciless desert of life, that it is not a soap bubble that bursts in our faces in the moment of death; you too will have the serenity of Jesus. You too will face death without fear.

II

If we really believe that life is eternal, it will take the sting out of death when it claims a loved one.

When Calvin Coolidge was in the White House, his young son died. The youth was at the dawn of a promising life. Both the President and Mrs. Coolidge were cast into deep grief. A year after the boy died, Mrs. Coolidge wrote an amazingly perceptive poem. In it she said:

> You, my son,
> Have shown me God.
> Your kiss upon my cheek
> Has made me feel the gentle touch
> Of Him who leads us on.
> The memory of your smile, when young,
> Reveals His face,
> As mellowing years come on apace.
> And when you went before,
> You left the gates of heaven ajar
> That I might glimpse,
> Approaching from afar,
> The glories of His grace.
> Hold, son, my hand,
> Guide me along the path,
> That, coming,
> I may stumble not,
> Nor roam,
> Nor fail to show the way
> Which leads us home.

141

For Mrs. Coolidge, the sting was gone from the death that claimed her son because she believed in eternal life.

I had a wonderful letter from a dear friend not long ago. His lovely wife had passed away. I had written him a note of sympathy and assurance of my prayers. He wrote to tell me of the five wonderful months he and his beloved had had after her apparent recovery from brain surgery. Then she became suddenly ill one night and she was gone in a matter of hours. He told how much he missed her and how the children had been magnificent through it all and how grateful he was for the wonderful years they had had together. Then he closed the letter in a most unusual way. He said, "Love from us *both*, and I do mean both, for Margie would want to be included."

Here is the instinct of a man who knows that life is eternal. Here is the natural expression of one who is confident that his beloved is too good to be through!

It takes the sting out of the mortal experience that removes a loved one from our physical presence when we really believe that death is only an incident and that life is eternal.

III

If we really believe that life is eternal, as Jesus believed it, we will have more respect for life.

If death is the end of us, then we must conclude that life has no ultimate value. If, on the other hand, death is a bridge over which we pass from mortal to immortal existence, then we are led to see that life must have a very great value. Otherwise, such a provision for its continuance would be utterly senseless.

What would be the use of trying to live the good life if the final victory belongs to death? Why should we try to be good? Why should we discipline ourselves to be honest and decent? If this life is all we have—if that's it and that's all there is to it—why shouldn't we extract every ounce of living for ourselves out of it as long as we can? Why should we deny ourselves anything? We live out our days, and we're through. The earth claims our bodies. We may live a while in someone's memory— then we're done—all washed up—exit and oblivion! Why exert ourselves to be somebody, to amount to something, to do anything but get all we can out of life if death is the end of it?

But what if the reverse is true? What if we have a whole eternity before us? What if there is a deathless quality about us, as Jesus obviously believed? What then? It will make a vast difference in the way we live!

Suppose you were a sculptor, and you were asked to carve a statue of a man. Would it make any difference to you if the material you were given to work with was only of temporary value? Suppose you were given a block of sandstone. You know that sandstone weathers with age. It finally will crumble, break off the edges, and wear away with the washing of rain and driving winds. Would you take careful pains with the figure if it were to be carved out of sandstone? But, suppose on the other hand you were given a block of marble

143

out of which to carve your statue. Would you not approach your task with the same careful devotion of a Michelangelo? Knowing that neither time nor the elements would deface your work, would you not seek to use chisel and hammer with patient discipline and skill?

Just so, if you believe that you are an eternal being, if you believe that your essential life is not limited to the time and space of earthly existence, you will treat your life with the respect it deserves. You will try to carve out something that is good and worthwhile.

Not only will this make a difference in our respect for ourselves, but it will also make a difference in the way we treat others.

It is interesting to watch a woman in her home when she is handling the dishes. The ordinary crockery from the breakfast table is handled without thought. She can be washing the breakfast dishes and be thinking of a thousand things—the news report on the radio, the new hat she has seen in the store window, the children's music lessons, her husband's hopes for advancement. She can even bounce an old jelly glass off the kitchen sink without batting an eye. But, let her be handling her best china and crystal, and she takes on a completely different manner! She is not lost in her dreams. She is thinking only of precious goblets and eggshell-thin china cups and saucers. She handles these things as lovingly as an artist touches a brush to canvas. There is a vast difference in the way you handle crockery and the way you handle china.

144

The way you treat persons depends upon your estimate of their value. If you have a low estimate of personality, you will treat people like crockery. If you have a high estimate of personality—if you think of persons as children of God with immortal souls—you will treat people like precious pieces of Dresden china.

When faith and immortality grow dim, man loses his concern for the right treatment of others. On the other hand, when man's faith in the eternal worth of persons becomes stronger, his treatment of his fellowman will step up to a new level. Can you consent to the assassination of a man's character if you believe that person to be a child of God and an immortal soul? Can you be unconcerned about the mass murder which is war if you believe the victims, whether they be on our side or the side of the so-called enemy, are precious in the sight of God? Will a man act in any way that would deny the dignity of a person of another race or color or national origin or class or anything else if he really believes that this person stands on the same level with him in the eyes of God—an eternal soul? Will a boy exploit a girl, or a girl a boy, for purposes of sex satisfaction if he or she really respects the other's personality as something God intends to live forever?

The way you treat another depends upon your estimate of that person's value, and to believe that person is an immortal soul is to invest such a one with the highest dignity and worth. The same is true of yourself. God has placed an unmistakable sign on every

145

person. It reads like this: "Priceless value. Handle with care!"

IV

If we really believe, as Jesus believed, in eternal life, it will give us a deeper understanding of the nature of God.

What kind of God would call us into being, permit us to begin our development as persons and to continue it through struggle and effort and pain, give us glimpses of possibilities beyond; only to let our growth be ruthlessly ended at death, as though it counted for nothing? It is difficult to think that God is like that! Such thinking about God reduces him to an impersonal force without heart.

When faith in immortality recedes, man's faith in a personal God who cares for him and loves him recedes with it.

Tennyson said:

> Thou wilt not leave us in the dust:
> Thou madest man, he knows not why,
> He thinks he was not made to die;
> And thou hast made him: thou art just.

In Olive Schreiner's *Story of an African Farm*, there is a scene in which Bonaparte comes upon the boy Waldo, who is playing with a little mechanical device that has taken nine months for him to build. He has put a lot of himself into his cherished creation. Bonaparte makes a show of interest in it and then in ruthless unconcern crushes the machine under his foot into the sand. A natural resentment wells up within us as we think of anyone as inhuman and unthinking as that.

Well, if we convince ourselves that there is no personal survival after death, then we must assume that God is a cosmic Bonaparte who has no real interest in us as individuals, who takes the fruits of our living, whether they be heroic or unheroic, and consents to their extinction as though they meant nothing. "What shall we say of the Power behind the universe," said Canon Streeter, "if it treats the individuality of heroic souls like oyster-shells at a banquet, whisked from the table to make room for the next course?"

When we really believe that life is eternal, then we cannot believe that God is some remote, impersonal force uninvolved in his creation. When we really believe that life is eternal, we really believe in a God who cares for each one of us.

Charles Rann Kennedy is one of my favorite playwrights. I had the privilege of a brief but close association with him before he died. He gave me all the books containing his plays and inscribed them thoughtfully with selected passages which meant so much to him. I cherish those books. They are among my most prized possessions. My favorite play of his is *The Terrible Meek*. It is a play written for three actors, and all the action until the very end is in the dark. There is a mother, whose son is hanging upon a cross above her. There is the captain, who has ordered his death, and a soldier, who executed the order. Through the long night there is conversation between the captain and the mother and the captain and the soldier. The agonized groans of the mother puncture the darkness. The captain comes to see the awful crime he has committed. The soldier never quite understands the agony of soul that is taking place in the captain's breast. In the final scene you begin to see the indistinct figures on the hilltop beneath the gaunt cross with the dead form upon it. The gray dawn is breaking. Instinctively you know that the sun is going to burst over the horizon in a moment. The soldier says to the captain, "Look, sir, wot did I tell yer? It's comin' light again." And the captain replies, "Eternally."

Discipleship Is Demanding

If any one comes to me and does not hate his own father and mother and wife and children and brothers and sisters, yes, and even his own life, he cannot be my disciple.

—Luke 14:26

Jesus was concerned about the great crowds that were following him. He was afraid they were shallow in their commitment to him. So, one day he gave them quite a shock. He said, "If any one comes to me and does not hate his own father and mother and wife and children and brothers and sisters, yes, and even his own life, he cannot be my disciple."

One can imagine the arched eyebrows when he said that. It didn't sound like Jesus. He never counseled anyone to hate. He bade them to love. Everyone knew how much he loved his own family. The people must have leaned forward to hear what he would say next. As if he hadn't made it plain enough, he followed the first shock treatment with another. "Whoever does not bear his own cross and come after me, cannot be my disciple."

These people were familiar with the sight of men carrying their crosses. Sepphoris was a town not far from Nazareth. When Jesus was a boy, Rome decided to make Sepphoris a new capital for the province. About this time someone started an ill-timed revolt against Rome. The Roman military determined to make Sepphoris an object lesson. Every man in the town was rounded up and nailed to a cross. Sepphoris must have been a forest of crosses. The people of Nazareth, not far away, could not have escaped the impact of the object lesson. Jesus, as a boy, certainly would have known about it. Perhaps he even went to see the grisly sight. Not only did this gory thing happen at Sepphoris. It happened at other places as well. Crosses were a familiar sight. Remember—this was before Jesus glorified the cross. You can imagine what an impression it made on the people to hear Jesus say, "Whoever does not bear his own cross and come after me, cannot be my disciple."

What did Jesus mean? He made it very plain in two parables. Suppose you are going to build a tower, he said. Wouldn't you sit down and count the cost to be sure you could complete it? Otherwise, the unfinished structure would stand there to mock you. Or, suppose you were a king and you were planning to make war upon your enemy. Wouldn't you carefully calculate your resources? And if you found yourself to be out-numbered, wouldn't you try to make peace with your enemy rather than to go against him with the sure prospect of defeat?

Both these parables make the same point. What Jesus was saying was: If you are going to follow me, you must count the cost. Put into the context of our own life today, Jesus was saying: Let no one fool himself. It costs something to be a Christian. Discipleship is demanding.

I

We know it costs terribly to be a Christian in some parts of the world today.

John Yue is a tailor in Hong Kong. He has prospered there. To see him today and to visit his fine establish-ment you would never dream that he was once a penniless refugee from Shanghai. He had been a very successful tailor in Shanghai. When the revolution came, he made a decision to leave Shanghai and the repressive restraints of the communist government. He came to Hong Kong with all his belongings in a suitcase. He left his wife and baby in Shanghai, intending to bring them out later. He walked the streets of Hong Kong, along with hundreds of thousands of other refugees. When he was nearly desperate, he encountered a sea captain for whom he had made suits in Shanghai many times. The captain was surprised to see him in Hong Kong. He ordered three suits. John borrowed equipment and supplies and made the suits for the captain. When he delivered them, his friend gave him a thousand dollars and encouraged him to use the money to set up his own business in Hong Kong. John Yue was one of the more fortunate of the refugees.

When he felt he was sufficiently established, John sent for his wife and son. It was a terrible ordeal waiting for them to come. Mrs. Yue made the mistake of trying to bring some money out of China. She was apprehended and questioned for two days. John said he spent those days in anxious prayer, hoping she and the baby would be all right. Finally, she was allowed to come through after the money had been taken from her. John is an usher at the Ward Memorial Methodist Church. Ninety percent of the people of that congregation are refugees. Being a Christian in Hong Kong is bad enough; being a Christian in Shanghai is even worse.

When I was on my way to the meeting of the Third Assembly of the World Council of Churches in New Delhi, India, I met a man who told me of a great Christian. He was a man of exceptional ability. He was offered the nomination for the vice-presidency of Burma. But a condition was attached to this offer. It would be necessary for him to renounce Christianity and to return to the state religion of Buddhism. The faithful Christian gentleman remained true to his faith and sacrificed the opportunity for national leadership. He paid a price for his discipleship.

Later, at New Delhi, I learned of a church rally

(Kirchentag) which was held in Berlin. It was decided to take some of the meetings into the Russian zone of Berlin. Bishop Dibelius of Germany was scheduled to be the speaker at one of these meetings. The church was crowded in East Berlin that day. Two thousand people stood outside, unable to get into the building. Since public worship is discouraged in the Eastern zone, government agents were in the crowd outside the church taking down the names of the people who had come to worship. An observer told of one young man who came over to one of these agents and said to him, "Be sure to get my name down!" And he gave him his name. Such is the courage of many Christians in East Berlin.

Leatrice Sakuma, a beautiful young Japanese girl, started attending the First Methodist Church of Honolulu when she was in high school. She joined the youth fellowship and eventually decided to become a Christian. The day she was baptized and joined the church she went home to find that her Buddhist parents, disapproving of her action, had placed her clothing on the front porch. This was mute evidence that they had disowned her. She picked up her belongings and went to the pastor's home. He and his wife took her into their home for a few days until she could get established in a location of her own. Later, they arranged for her to come to the mainland and go to school. She graduated with honors and returned to Hawaii as a Christian missionary.

Dean and Elsie Freudenberger are missionaries in the

Congo. Dean is a graduate of an agricultural school, and he is trying to teach the Congolese the methods of agriculture and animal husbandry that will enable them to raise their meager standard of living and overcome the malnutrition that besets so many of these people. When the terrible civil strife broke out in the Congo shortly after that nation achieved its independence, Dean and Elsie Freudenberger were caught at their post. Their lives were in danger. After the wave of horror passed, the Freudenbergers came home on furlough. When their furlough period had ended, they returned to the Congo. Their life is hard. They live in the midst of danger. They have paid a great price for their discipleship.

Yes, in many places in our world it costs heavily to be a Christian.

II

When I think of how little it costs us to be Christians, I am ashamed.

In his book *The Noise of Solemn Assemblies*, Peter Berger writes about the religious establishment in America. By this he means "religion established securely and in a taken-for-granted manner as an important institution of American society."

It is true that religion occupies a prominent place in our life in this land. Being a church member is the thing to do. It must be, since two thirds of the people do it! We have a little flurry once in a while about separation of church and state and prayer and Bible reading in public schools, but for the most part Americans are committed to the idea that religion is an important part of our heritage and tradition. We have a religious slogan on our coinage. Churches are encouraged by tax exemption. Politicians are careful to instruct their speech writers to put a quotation from the Bible and a reference to the providence of God into their campaign speeches. Without apology, we refer to our nation as being "under God." We are careful to open our conventions, our service clubs, and other important community activities with an invocation.

The Christian church is a part of the American way of life. I lived in a certain city when it celebrated its seventy-fifth anniversary. They had a parade through the streets. At the head of that parade was what they called "the march of the churches." Selected young people carried the Christian and the American flags side by side. The Council of Churches was represented with a float. Many individual churches participated in like manner. This was very appropriate for that town, for it had been noted through the years as a city of churches.

In this kind of setting where church membership is universally approved, the cost of being a Christian is not very great. There is no government official in a Sunday morning church service to give people a black mark for being in church. In some places a man attends public worship at the risk of losing his job or being discriminated against for good job opportunities, but not in America! In fact, in this country it is usually regarded as an asset for a business or professional person or a politician to be seen in church. No one here faces the prospect of having to submit to the demands of some little caesar requiring him to sign a paper denying everything he holds dear in his faith. Few of us have had to cut ourselves off from our families as Leatrice Sakuma did to become a Christian. There are those who have suffered for conscience' sake, to be sure, in the civil rights movement, as conscientious objectors to war, at the hands of McCarthyism—but these are few and far between in the ranks of millions of church members in our society.

If Christ were to come into the church some Sunday morning and show his bleeding hands and ask of the people, "What have you done for me lately?" I wonder what the reply would be. Perhaps someone would say, "I went to church an average of once a month last year!" Another might say, "I served on a committee to plan a Sunday school class party!" Someone else might say, "I put a dollar bill in the collection plate every time I come to church!"

When I think of how little is required of Christians in America, I am ashamed that we can't somehow match the discipleship of the Christians in East Berlin, in Shanghai, in Moscow, in Rangoon, in the Congo. But then—perhaps we can!

III

We must wrench ourselves out of our indulgence in what some have called "easy Christianity." To do this

we must observe two things which have always charac-
terized true discipleship.

First, we must honestly care about people. In Sep-
tember of 1964 *Look* magazine had a penetrating article
entitled "Who Cares?" The article recounted some of
the startling evidences of human apathy in our society.
It told of a shocking event in New York City. It was
3:25 a.m. A twenty-eight-year-old woman was going
home from work. She was attacked and stabbed. She
screamed for help and her attacker fled. But when no
one responded to the woman's cries, he returned and
stabbed her again. He continued to knife her until she
died. Later it was found that there were thirty-eight people who had heard her cry for help, but none of them
came to her rescue. No one even bothered to call the
police.

Here is an excerpt from the article.

In Chicago, sixty persons ignored the uniformed police-
man's cries for assistance as he battled two youths. In
Santa Clara, California, several motorists saw a taxicab
driver being robbed, but none even summoned police. In
San Pedro, California, other motorists drove by two police-
men struggling to prevent a man from jumping off a 185-
foot-high bridge. "We were hanging on for dear life and
trying to get someone to stop. But they all drove on like
they didn't want to be bothered or get involved," one of the
patrolmen reported later. Back in New York City, a Broadway
crowd stood by while eight men stomped two; a Bronx
crowd would not rescue a naked girl from a rapist's attack,
and bystanders fled from a 19 year old college student who

What Jesus Proclaimed

had just been stabbed by a member of a gang of toughs. His statement to the *New York Times* is unforgettable: "I put my hand down and saw blood, I went over to a car that had stopped to watch. 'Please help me to a hospital,' I said. They rolled up their windows and drove away. . . . Nobody on the street helped me."

Jesus made it very plain that a condition of discipleship was to care about people. He told the unforgettable story about the Samaritan who responded to the need of a beaten and bruised man by the side of the road. The point of this parable is that loving God and loving your neighbor are all of one piece, and a person's neighbor is a man in need whoever and wherever he is. As Professor Milo Connick says about this parable, "The cost of discipleship is love without limit."

Jesus told another story about the Son of man sitting in judgment upon all people. He described the division as a shepherd separating the sheep from the goats. One group was accepted and blessed because they ministered to the needy and the afflicted. The other group was condemned because they did not.

One of the demands of discipleship is that we must care about people who are in need. We must be willing to get involved. We must quit praying, "Use me, O Lord, use me—but only in an advisory capacity!" There is a cross in caring for people. When we get involved in helping people in need, we stand a good chance of getting hurt. But this is one of the demands of discipleship.

The other great demand of discipleship is that we honestly care about Christ. If one is to be a disciple, he must be faithful to his Master. This means being obedient to his commands. It means abiding by his teachings. If we honestly care about Christ, we will live what he taught. Saying, "Lord, Lord!" will not do. Lip service is the ultimate blasphemy.

Peter Berger says that the typical church member leads a double life. When he leaves home in the morning, "he leaves behind him the person that played with the children, mowed the lawn, chatted with the neighbors—and went to church. His actions now become dominated by a radically different logic—the logic of business, industry, politics, or whatever other sector of public life the individual is related to. In this second life of his the church is totally absent." If we have found Christianity easy, either we are living this double life or we have misunderstood the meaning of discipleship. Dietrich Bonhoeffer, who was executed at Flossenburg concentration camp in Germany in 1945, left us a theological and literary heritage in a book called *The Cost of Discipleship*. He saw discipleship as an "exclusive attachment" to the person of Christ. This is the second and greatest demand of discipleship.

If we love Jesus, we will do what he says!

At first the requirements of discipleship seem like impossible demands; later, when one has passed through the discipline of obedience to the grace of faith, discipleship becomes not a burden but a priceless privilege.